To Tony Gledhill.

The History of Hilston Park

in the parish of St Maughans
and the county of Monmouthshire

1293 - 2011

Pamela Pugh.

by Pamela Pugh

∞ Published by Ladehouse Books ∞

First published March 2012 by Ladehouse Books Publishing
www.Ladehousebooks.co.uk

A Catalogue record of this book is available from the British Library.

ISBN 978-0-9571729-0-6

Set in 12pt Palatino and printed in England by Orphans Press Ltd.,
Arrow Close, Leominster Enterprise Park, Leominster,
Herefordshire HR6 0LD.

Email your memories to info@hilstonpark.co.uk
or read any feedback to the book at www.hilstonpark.co.uk/feedback

Contents

Part 5   **A new era begins**

MAPS

PHOTOGRAPHS

All other pictures; ©Desmond Pugh Photography

Dedicated to my five grandchildren,
Henry and Oliver Pugh, Louise, Hannah and Andrew Pritchard

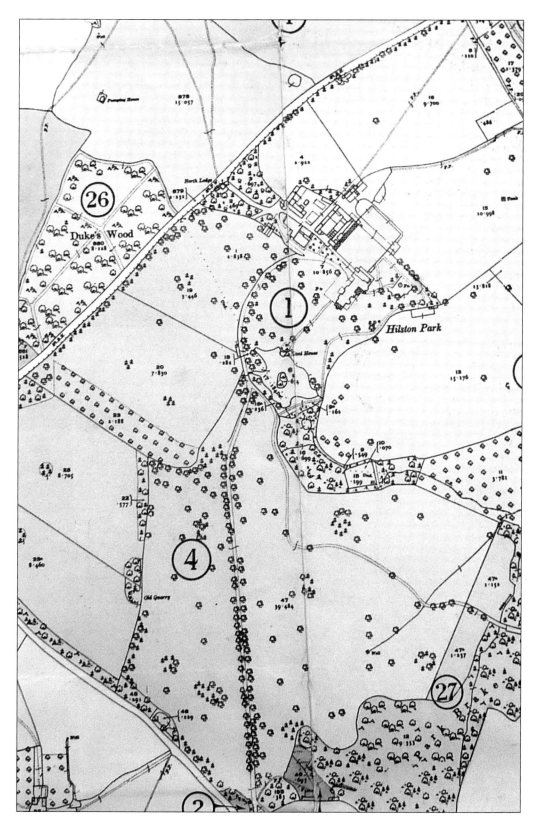

Acknowledgments

A book such as this relies a lot upon the assistance of others. Although I spent many hours researching and compiling the information into handwritten notes, I could not have completed this unique reference without the help of the following:

Vernon Pugh, my husband who has lived around this area longer than most people; his local knowledge has helped make this book what I hope will be an authoritative reference. *Desmond Pugh*, whose library of photographs help illustrate this history, without his help with the text and the page layout, my patience may well have been exhausted many months ago. *Simon Cropper*, for his expertise in copy-editing. *Louise Pritchard*, my granddaughter, who helped me with the many additions that I kept finding. *Betty Williams* of The Local History Centre for her tireless work looking through old copies of the *Monmouthshire Beacon* and *The Merlin*. *Dr Eric Old*, of Castle Museum, Monmouth, for his help. *Charles Graham* of Usk, for the loan of the Grahams' family book, his family owned Hilston from 1873 to 1918. *Charles and Lyn Blacklock*, for manuscripts and maps relating to the estate of T E Davies, who bought the Hilston Estate in 1947. *Janet Pugh* and *Phyllis Williams*, (Norton Court) for their assistance in proofing this book, and to Phyllis for sharing the wisdom of her experience with local history books. Friends and neighbours, who have lent me books, given advice and allowed us to copy photographs over the years, enabling me to have such an extensive history of the building. These include: *Henry Edwards, Bill Price, Mike Oxford, Bryn Tucker, Colin Perrott, Dorothy (Dolly) Morgan* formerly of the Waen, *Josephine Higginbotham (née Morgan), Glyn and Dan Williams, Jean Blakesley (née Wraight) Delia Nash, Jean Ridley (daughter of Phyllis Gordon)* and *Judith McConnel*. *Irene Williams (née Lawrence)*; her father and grandfather worked on the estate, she was a housemaid and her husband was the footman; she was able to furnish many of the details of life around Hilston Park when it was still a country estate.

Also *Ian Kennett* and the staff at Hilston Park, for their kindness in allowing me access to the building, above ground and below, to bring the record up to the present day, also *Jan Evans*, who lent me information about Hilston, and other staff, past and present. The *Monmouthshire Beacon* for use of their time and resources. *The British Museum, CADW* and *Parks and Gardens Data Services* for allowing me to reproduce their material. The widow of *Jack Axten* for allowing me access to his extensive records of St Maughans.

Last, but not least, *Richard Gledhill* who encouraged me to write a history of Hilston Park in the first place.

It has taken me longer than I anticipated to write this book, with all the disruptions and interruptions of a normal family life.

Pamela Pugh, 2012

Preface (by Phyllis Williams)

The author of this authoritative publication on The Hilston Park Estate in Monmouthshire, is a passionate countrywoman. Pam Pugh spent her childhood on her family's farm in Herefordshire, marriage then brought her to her husband's family farm in the neighbouring county of Monmouthshire. Since 1958 Pam and her husband Vernon, have lived and farmed at the Home Farm, formerly part of the Hilston Park Estate and adjacent to the beautiful mansion house of Hilston Park.

As well as her love of the countryside, Pam has a passion for history and especially for the history of her surroundings. For many years, she has been collecting photographs of the area, principally of the parishes of Skenfrith and St Maughan's. Living next door to the house of Hilston Park has given a focus to her research and Pam has been able to trace the owners and occupiers of Hilston from medieval times to 1948, when the estate was sold and the house itself acquired by Monmouthshire County Council to serve as a school for pupils with special needs and, since 1971, as an Educational Outdoor Centre to serve the county. The second part of the book is devoted to social life in the district, some of which centred on the Hilston Estate and include memories of local pastimes.

Many books have been read and consulted, documents deciphered, local residents interviewed and past residents and their relatives contacted, together with past and present staff at Hilston Park. The result is this fascinating and informative book, with which so many people have been involved. In addition to her own collection of photographs and illustrations, Desmond, Pam's son, has contributed many photographs most of which have been taken to illustrate the text and which help the reader to appreciate the splendour of the house and surrounding buildings.

PDW
Norton Court
January 2012

Part 1

Introduction

Hilston Park, Monmouthshire

This grand house has been known as Old Hilston, Upper Hilston and Hilston House, but since the 1840s it has been called Hilston Park. The imposing house that stands on the site today is at least the fourth that can be accounted for; how many dwellings have stood here between 1293, the first time it was mentioned (as Hild's Place) in the Lancaster Survey of that year, and 1600, is unknown.

Hilston House has probably one of the best sites in Monmouthshire. It stands in the parish of St. Maughan's, six miles north east of the county town of Monmouth.

To the east is the boundary with the county of Herefordshire, marked by the River Monnow. Llangattock-Vibon-Avel lies to the south west of the house, with Skenfrith to the north east. The best view is from the south side; it looks over the beautiful valley of the Monnow towards the Maypole and St Maughans parish. On a clear day one can see the pretty church of St Meugan, where some of the owners of Hilston are buried.

An aerial picture, taken in 1967 by Skyviews, showing the north west aspect of the house and the North Lodge, (bottom centre-left) with the twin pillars either side of the entrance. The Home Farm and its buildings are in the centre of the picture

Apart from its lovely setting and beautiful frontage, the house has many other great advantages. The entrance hall and stairs with its old oak panelling sets the tone of this well planned and spacious house.

The conservatory to the rear of the house, facing south towards Monmouth

Interior views of the house showing some of the murals, ornate ceilings and the fireplaces which survive to present day, the picture inset, shows the former Drawing Room fireplace

The rooms are not too big - which adds to their charm - both downstairs and upstairs are level floors, with relatively easy access to all the rooms. The servants' quarters, rebuilt around 1912 by the Grahams, blend well with the main house. On the north side of the building was a well with a pump; an addition to the water supply from the well beneath the house. A plinth now marks the spot, covered by an ornamental flower container. There are also underground soft water tanks,

one is in the annex to the vegetable garden, with at least three at the Home Farm. During the time of the Grahams, a system was installed to pump the water into the tanks at the top of the house. This water came from a well in the field opposite the North Lodge. The two lodges are much later additions to the house and were rebuilt by Douglas Graham in 1912.

On the north east side of the house are the servants' quarters added in 1912, and a Mexican Bean tree

This 1967 picture, taken by Skyviews, shows the southerly side of the house looking towards St Maughans; the two temporary classrooms (1); the Copper Beech tree in front of the house (2) - cut down in the 1990s following a structural survey; the Stableblock (3) - demolished in the 1970s a few years after this picture was taken - stood on the far side of The Barracks, itself demolished in 1936. The gardens and the greenhouses (4) are to the right of the house extending to the right hand side of the picture. The buildings belonging to the Home Farm (5) begin at the back of the greenhouses and extend to the top yard (6). The garage that once served Hilston (7) is now part of the farm. The remains of the Italian Garden are at (8), but the Icehouse (9), and Summerhouse (10) no longer exists. The Home Farm house (11) was once the Bothy and the head gardener's accommodation

The remains of the Italian Garden

The grounds extend to around 15 acres and include some magnificent trees, including a Mexican Bean, Wellingtonia, Cedar of Lebanon, Lime, Copper Beech and Monkey Puzzle; the former vegetable garden is now an orchard. On the west side, about 50 yards from the house, is a lake with two islands. In former times it had a small boat house with stained glass windows; this was demolished in the late 1950s. Features on the south side before 1945 included a rose garden and sunhouse with a path to steps, still visible today, leading to two tennis courts in the field overlooking St Maughans. Not far from the summerhouse, looking towards Crossways, was an icehouse; this no longer exists. All that could denote its position many years ago was a mound of earth with steps dug out of one side.

The lake panorama, top picture, shows the two islands and the lower picture, taken in the dry spell in 2011, reveals the stone revetted wall built to create and contain the lake.

Part 2

Beginnings

1293 - 1606
and
Lower Hilstone

The early days

The first mention of a dwelling at Hilston is in the *Lancaster Survey* of 1293, which refers to a smallholding called Hild's Place; Hild is an old English name. Hild's tun (meaning Hild's farm) may well be the origin of the name Hilston. Other sources refer to this site as home of Mathio de Hildeston, and it is this name that is marked on the 14th century map seen here. Very

few early facts about Hilston can be found. After the 1300s, apart from the name Mathio de Hildeston, the next two recorded names are mentioned in the *Lancaster Survey* of the 1600s: Jacob Hilston and the Barrie or Barry family. However, the wider local history of the area, from the beginning of Norman occupation to the more prosperous times, is well documented.

Life during the 13th, 14th and 15th centuries was a time of upheaval in the area around St Maughans and Hilston. By the early 1200s, the Normans had colonised most of England and Wales, and the castles of Grosmont, Whitecastle and Skenfrith are proof that they had a very strong presence in the area near Hilston. The manorial system they imposed on the old Welsh structure brought huge changes to the countryside and social life over the next two centuries. Norman knights were given small estates and set up fortified houses to provide security against the native population. The moats of two such houses can be seen today in St Maughans at Tregate and at Newcastle, to the rear of Newcastle Farm.

Life under the Normans was fairly peaceful at first, but the 14th and 15th centuries brought a series of disasters. Between 1309 and 1312, a succession of bad harvests caused years of scarcity and hunger, made worse still from 1315 to 1317 by the Great Famine that affected much of northern Europe. There was a heavy loss of people and cattle, the latter dying of malnutrition. The scale of the famine left the population severely weakened, and there were fewer people to cultivate the land. Then in 1348, came the first outbreak of the Black Death, recorded as one of the deadliest plagues in history. The initial recovery was short-lived, for the disease reappeared in 1361 and 1369. It is estimated that over 20 per cent of the local population died.

Eventually, the countryside and inhabitants around Hilston returned to normal. Unfortunately, 1402 brought the rebellion of Owain Glyndwr, another blow that affected much of the countryside, including St Maughans. Glyndwr's revolt proved devastating for the people of Wales. Chroniclers reported that Glyndwr 'brought all things to waste' and the English king 'proclaimed havoc in Wales'. The rebellion was accompanied by an extensive destruction of villages and the mills by both sides in 1404 to deny the enemy the means to feed an army. 'Normal economic life and civil administration ceased for several years, and as late as 1420 it was reported that St Maughans was lying wholly in decay';[1] this probably included Hilston. During the Glyndwr rebellion, his followers fought and defeated the English at Craig-y-Dorth, near Cwmcarvan, Monmouthshire, in 1404 when they chased the English soldiers back to the gates of Monmouth Castle. In the Spring of 1405 they marched on Grosmont and burned most of the town to the ground. During this time, it is possible they used the old pre-toll roads in the area between St Maughans and Crossways, which links the area to Grosmont, coming close to the early Hilston site as they ransacked the country around this area.

Charles Coxe, in volume two of *An historical tour in Monmouthshire*, 1801, talks of the roads in the area in chapter 34:

> The horseway leaves the carriage road about four miles from Monmouth, and after traversing St. Maughan's Common, proceeds through a narrow steep and stony lane, overgrown with thickets, and pitched with large stones placed edgeways in the boggy soil; these stones being broken or displaced, a succession of uneven steps is formed, and horses, not accustomed to such rugged and miry ways, are continually apt to stumble and flounder.

1. Monmouth Borough Archives, from Jack Axten's leaflet on St Maughans Church

The picture shows Coxstone in the foreground, with The Upper Grove at the middle left and the hamlet of Crossways at the back to the right of the picture. The old road took this route, as marked on the map opposite. This view is from St Maughans Church

Vernon Pugh, who farms the former parkland of Hilston, can remember the old road:

> At Crossways, the road continued on past Laun and Deri, and Park Cottages across the Dingle field, through the hollow of the next field, running underneath where the pylons cross the field, to where the stream goes into White House Farm boundary; a footpath bridge is there now. The road was just a sunken earth road, about six feet deep; you could stand in there and not see over the top.

The 1500s brought further – albeit less catastrophic – change to the area. The Acts of Union, passed between 1536 and 1543, imposed English law and taxes on Wales, and affected many landholdings and ownerships. Henry VIII incorporated Wales into England - the future owners of Hilston would have regarded themselves as living in England - and Gwent became Monmouthshire. Following this, the country was referred to as Wales and Monmouthshire.

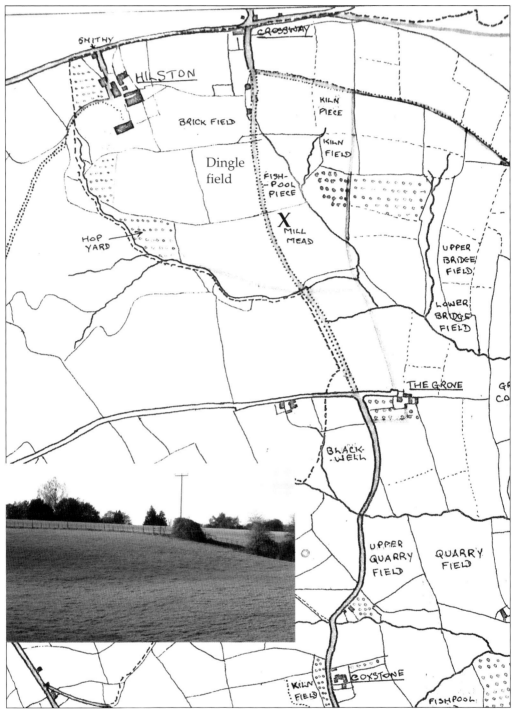

This 1861 map showing the old road coming through Crossways (top) between Upper and Lower Grove, on through to Coxstone and continuing to St Maughans. The inset picture shows the path of the sunken road, now filled in, from just below the bushes on the right crossing the picture to the lower left. This area is marked X on the map above and on the picture left. Hilston behind the trees top left

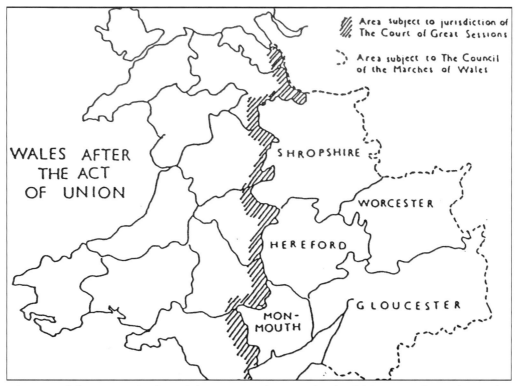

As part of the reorganisation of the country the Marcher lordships were formed into the counties of Brecon, Denbigh, Montgomery, Radnor and Monmouth, which along with all eight existing shires of Wales, were to be incorporated, united and annexed with Henry VIII's Realm of England

In the *Survey of the Duchy of Lancaster 1609-13* we find the first mention of Thomas Hilston. Roughly translated from the Latin, it states:

> By the custom of the manor according to the supply of eight acres of arable land and pasture… in St Maughans… of the late Thomas James Hilston, his father, and pays rent amounting to twelve pence Richard Barry and John Barry hold them and their heirs according to the custom of the manor was called one meadow containing Garled Hilston… twenty acres in St Maughan… lately of John Barry, their father, and they pay rent amounting to 12 pence.

Richard and John Barry are without doubt two of the sons of John Barry of Skenfrith and Elizabeth (née Coxe), daughter of Hugh Coxe of Hilston. They are believed to be family descendants of Owain Glyndwr.[2]

2. John Burke *Genealogical and Heraldic History of the Commoners of Great Britain and Ireland*

Owain Glyndwr

§

Sir John Scudamore m. Elsbeth aka Alys ferch Owain, daughter of above

§

John Pye m. Elizabeth Scudamore of Kentchurch, daughter of above

§

Jenkin Pye, son of above

§

William Vaughan (Llanrothal) m. Mawd Pye (Saddlebow),[3] daughter of above

§

Phillip ap John (Skenfrith) m. *Unknown* Vaughan, daughter of above

§

William Barry (Skenfrith) m. Joan ferch Phillip (Skenfrith), daughter of above

§

John Barry, son of above m. Elizabeth Coxe, daughter of Hugh Coxe of Hilston

It is this last name, Coxe, that firmly establishes the first recorded reference to Hilston in *Llyfr Baglan*,[4] page 162. Documents from shortly after this period mention the Coxe (or Cox, Cocks or Cockes) family. A map on display in Skenfrith Church, dating from around 1580, shows Norton Court, one mile north of Hilston and southwest of Skenfrith (known at the time as Ould Courte), to have been the house of Charles Coxe and family, who lived here until the end of the 16th century.

Arms of Cox

Wilhelmina Jackson, who lived at Blackbrooke, near Skenfrith, wrote a book titled *Bygone Days in the March Wall of Wales* in 1926 under the pen name M.N.J. On page 10, she mentions an entry for Skenfrith dated 22nd May 1580, discovered in the Court Rolls of the Duchy of Lancaster, listing what Juliana Cockes had inherited on the death of her father. The properties mentioned include:

> Norton (Court), Walston (Walson), Tyre-gaute (Tre-Gout), Tyre-Gwyn (White House?), Ostery, Treheron (Trevonny?) and Ales Barkyte.

The last name possibly relates to Norton Chapel fields, as a number of these places were part of the Norton Court Estate as recorded in later years. Some of these place-names later appear on the Hilston Estate.

3. Now the Mynde, Much Dewchurch, Herefordshire. Saddlebow was the hill above it
4. John Williams (1910) *Llyfr Baglan* 1600-1607

The Cox family had a considerable estate and were important local gentry; Bradney [5] quotes a William Coxe living in the Parish of St Maughans with a tenement and lands in 1606, members were still living in the area in the 17th century.

An old road out of Hilston was from the southwest side of the house across the park to The Grove; joining the road to St Maughans at the old highway which leads from Norton and Crossways to St Maughans Church. At this junction is a farm now called Coxstone (Coxe's settlement?), a possible legacy of the Coxe family.

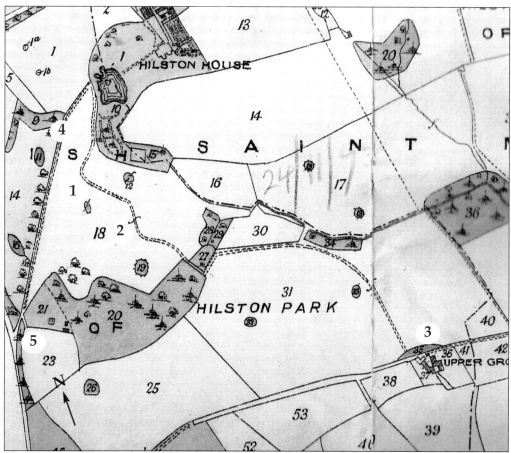

This 1843 tithe map shows the old road running south initially (1) and then southeast of the mansion house (2) towards Upper Grove (3) and on to St Maughans. A later drive was taken across the park (4) to join the Monmouth to Newcastle toll road. The South Lodge - originally a round building - was built at this junction with the road (5) and the newly created entrance to Hilston Park.

5. Joseph Bradney (1904) *The Hundred of Skenfrith*,

The Barries (or Barrys) lived at Skenfrith House (now demolished), close to the site of what is now The Farm, Newcastle, half a mile southwest of Hilston. They were also regarded as landed gentry with considerable standing in the community. Another branch of this family lived at Tregate, near Llanrothal. These two families are mentioned in both *Llyfr Baglan 1600-1607*, compiled by John Williams in 1910 and the 1904 book by Joseph Bradney, *The Hundred of Skenfrith*. Llyfr Baglan shows the Barrie family tree on page 162.

John Barrie
m. sole heir to the estate in Skenfrith.

§

Jenkin Barrie
m. Jane Herbert, descendant from William, Earl of Pembroke.

§

William Barry
m. Joan ferch Phillip

§

John Barrie
m. Elizabeth, daughter to Hugh Coxe of Hilston, St Maughans.

This last reference, reveals the links the two families had to Hilston and each other. Hilston by now would have been a substantial residence. Before we move to the next owner of Hilston, it is worth looking at a list of farms and holdings around the date of 1606 belonging to the estate at that time. It consists of Blackmores Farm, St Maughans; Cox's Farm; Pontyrehen Farm, Llanvihangel-Ystern-Llewern;[6] a messuage (or holding) called Penyrhewll, Llangattock-Vibon-Avel; a messuage at Lower Crossways;[7] and three messuages with Smith's Forge and appurtenances. Also:

> All that part and division of the tithe of all sorts of grain heretofore belonging to the Chapel of Llanvaire Gilgoes and part of the possessions of the late Monastery of Dore.[8]

The possessions mentioned above possibly refer to land belonging to Grace Dieu Abbey that lies three miles south west from Hilston in the parish of Llanvihangel-Ystern-Llewern. Dore Abbey, Herefordshire was the mother church of Grace Dieu.

6. It is this farm that the Needhams, page 32, already owned; they built a house there for a family member and it is this building that stands today.
7. Curiously enough this was the name for the Old Boot in the 17th century
8. Fred Levett (1984) The Story of Skenfrith, Grosmont and St Maughans

Aristocratic connections

The area around Hilston has had aristocratic links for centuries. Edward I had many lordships in Monmouthshire, including Monmouth. In 1264, lordships of Monmouth passed to Edmund Crouchback when he was created Earl of Lancaster and for several centuries they were part of the great Lancastrian estates.

In 1492, Charles Somerset (1460-1526) married Elizabeth Herbert, the only daughter and sole heir of William, Earl of Huntingdon; she brought him vast areas of land in both Monmouthshire and Wales. The dissolution of the monasteries brought more land into the estate, including Tintern Abbey and Parc Grace Dieu Abbey. According to the Monmouth historian Keith Kissack, the Somersets bought the Duchy of Lancaster land in 1631, making the holding around Monmouth one vast estate. Henry Somerset (1629-1700), was made 1st Duke of Beaufort in 1682 after the Restoration. This Monmouthshire estate then dominated the parishes of St Maughans, Llangattock and Skenfrith. The Beaufort name subsequently appears in a variety of documents to do with the ownership of Hilston or matters of copyhold, and on many maps of the area.

Norton Court, one mile west of the village of Skenfrith, Monmouthshire

On the 15th August, 1854, properties still owned by the Duke of Beaufort were auctioned and included:

Norton Farm, 315 acres; Barn Farm, 70 acres; Tyr Gaut, (Tre Gout) 96 acres: Woodside, 106 acres; Little Demesne, 95 acres; Upper House, 48 acres; Lyvos, 204 acres and Placivor, 246 acres, (Cross Ash); Porthgwin Cottage and the Blacksmith's Shop (Brynderi road out of Cross Ash).[1]

Lyvos, now Great Lyvos, Cross Ash,
with a well house in the foreground

John Hamilton, page 62, took the opportunity to enlarge the Hilston Estate around 1865 by purchasing some of those properties that were not sold in 1854 and still for sale. Property in the area which was still owned by the ninth Duke of Beaufort in the early 1900s included the Hill Farm (now called White House Farm, Crossways), and Norton Court. In Kelly's Directory of 1901, the Duke of Beaufort is noted as being Lord of the Manor of Grosmont, Skenfrith and St Maughan's. The wood opposite Hilston's North Lodge was once called Tregout Wood; this subsequently changed to Duke's Wood.

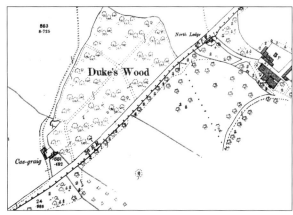

Map from a Blackbrooke Estate catalogue,
before 1921, showing Duke's Wood

1. From the Deeds of the Home Farm

Lower Hilston

A small estate that was known as Lower Hilston or Little Hilston, midway between Laundry Cottage (now Laun and Deri), Crossways and the Lower Grove, no longer exists. All that now remains is a well and an old stone bridge, pictured below.

Lower Hilston was the residence of Thomas Phillips, rector of Grosmont and Llanfoyst (Llanfoist) in the eighteenth century; his son Herbert also lived there. When the family died out, the house and land became part of Upper Hilston. This must have occurred before 1861 since Lower Hilston appears on the Upper Hilston Estate papers of that year.

Upper Hilston, briefly, became Hilston House. The 107 acres became part of the deer park, built by George Cave. Later the land, along with 31 acres at the Green Farm, was incorporated into the adjacent Hill Farm, now White House, Crossways.

Thomas Phillips and his wife, Joyce, went to Llanrothal Church, taking the lane through Hill Farm to Ruthlin Mill, using stepping stones to cross the river Monnow. Mary Hopson, in her book, *A Wander Round Llanrothal*, talks of seeing the remains of a medieval weir and Jack Axten speculates on the existence of a Roman crossing place between Tregate Bridge and Llanrothal and said that a cobbled way can still be seen.[1]

At the closest point of the river to Llanrothal Church there is an obstruction in the river

Thomas Phillips and his wife, Joyce, were buried at Llanrothal Church. Mary Hopson records in her book that Joyce's tomb (a granddaughter of Sir Thomas Herbert of Wonastow) is by the south wall of the chancel; burial records state that the 'wife of Thomas Phillips, clerk of Grismond (Grosmont), was buried in 1737'. Mary Hopson also records a Thomas Phillips 'of Lower Hillston, Clerk, M.A., rector of Grosmont and Lanfoyst in the county of Monmouth, who departed this life Sept. 3rd 17...'.[2]

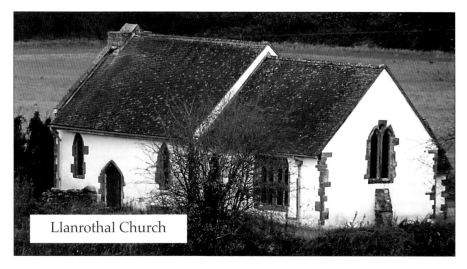

Llanrothal Church

1. The unpublished works of Jack Axten
2. Mary Hopson (1987) *A Wander Round Llanrothal*

The interior of the 12th century church at Llanrothal

THE LITTLE GRAVE
IMMEDIATELY BENEATH,
IS DEVOTED TO THE REMAINS OF
CATHERINE, THE WIFE OF
CHARLES NOSWORTHY MICHELL,
CLERK, MASTER OF ARTS,
OF BRUTON IN THE COUNTY OF SOMERSET,
VICAR OF THIS AND LLANGATTOCK PARISHES
DAUGHTER OF
HERBERT PHILLIPS, ESQUIRE,
OF LOWER HILSTON.

TRIFLING ARE THE DATES OF TIME,
WHEN THE SUBJECT IS ETERNITY

AND ALSO TO THE REMAINS OF THE SAID
CHARLES NOSWORTHY MICHELL.

Herbert Phillips is buried in St Maughans Church, his wall memorial can be found on the left hand side of the altar.

His daughter's memorial is on the right, opposite.

There are memorial stones in Llangattock-Vibon-Avel churchyard to John and Jane Roberts, of Lower Hilston, who died in 1819 and 1843 respectively.

According to the unpublished work of Jack Axten, one of the flagstones in the nave is of Robert Blake of Upper Hilston died January 18th, 1824 and buried on 23rd February

PEDIGREE OF THE FAMILY OF PHILLIPS, LOWER HILSTON [2]

James Phillips, Vicar of Skenfrith
married Jane, daughter of unknown
§
Thomas Phillips, rector Grosmont and Llanfoist
m.Joyce, daughter of Timothy Britton of Wrestlingworth
§
Herbert Phillips*
m. Mary, daughter of Thomas Evans of Llangattock-Vibon-Avel
§
Thomas Phillips, Attorney and Town Clerk, Monmouth
died without issue

*Other children of Herbert included;
Anne Marie, *d. infancy*
Rev. Charles Phillips, *1771-1818, no issue*
William *d. unknown*
Mary *d. unknown*
Sarah *d. aged 11*
Charles Phillips, *Vicar of LVA, Raglan, St Maughans, Llandenny, d. without issue*
James *d. aged 15*
Catherine (1769-1821) *m. Charles Michell, no known issue*

2. John Burke, *Genealogical and Heraldic History of the Commoners of Great Britain and Ireland*

*The memorial to James Phillips lies on the right hand side of the altar,
pictured here in St Bridget's Church, Skenfrith, Monmouthshire*

Lower Hilstone used to stand where an oak tree now grows. Top picture, the site, left of centre, looking east and the line of the National Grid. Above, from the site looking south; The Grove is top right, with St Maughans in the background

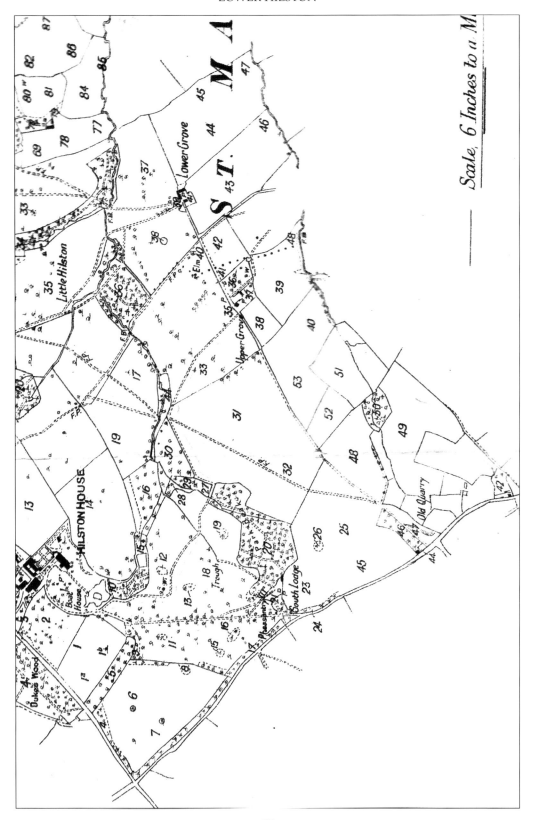

Scale, 6 Inches to a M.

Part 3

The Occupants

1660 - 1947

The Needham family c.1660 - 1803

Around 1660, Sebastian Needham (c.1630-1667) settled in the area. The Needhams were a Catholic family, and Sebastian's descendants were listed in the *Recusant Rolls* [1] from 1679 onwards. A Robert Needham was recorded in Catholic records as living at the Grange House, Llanfair Cilgoed from 1673 to 1683. Near the end of the 17th century, the Needhams acquired (Upper) Hilston. Whether it was this first Sebastian who built the house that later burnt down, (page 54), is not clear. There was no mention of the property by name in a survey carried out in the early 17th century, but the surname Hilston was noted as a smallholder.

By family tradition, most of the male Needhams became lawyers or priests. As Catholics, they were restricted in how they could practice as attorneys, not being legally qualified. But they continued to advise their Catholic neighbours on points of law, despite these restrictions, and helped in the preparing of deeds and wills. Other members of the Needham family included a Franciscan, a Jesuit, and three secular priests. The Jesuit was Father Sebastian Needham, a son of Robert and Susan, born at Hilston in 1671.

The first Sebastian Needham did not own the estate for long however, he died on 26th March 1667 and was buried at Skenfrith Church. He never married. The estate was inherited by his (illegitimate?) son Robert, who married Susan, daughter of Turberville Morgan of Llanfair Cilgoed. Robert died in 1723, and his wife died in 1739. In his will, he named his wife Susan, his son Sebastian (his other son, Robert having pre-deceased him) and daughters Ursula and Susan. He bequeathed his law books to his grandsons so they could 'choose a profession to avoid idleness and bad company' and asked for 'burial in a frugal and decent manner at night-time'[2] in accordance with the usual procedure during penal times. Susan died aged 99 and left £5 in her will so that each poor Catholic at her funeral would receive a shilling, and other poor people sixpence each.

1. The Recusant Rolls of the Exchequer are annual rolls of sheriffs' accounts, they relate the Catholic recusants' fines and forfeitures and are preserved at the Public Record Office
2. Catholic Registers of 1715

The Robert that pre-deceased them, married firstly Lucy Scudamore of Blackbrooke in 1700, and then secondly Anne, daughter of Edward Pye of the Mynde, Much Dewchurch, Herefordshire. In 1717, Robert and Anne were indicted;

> for not coming to their Parish Church of St Maughans or any other church or chapel or usual place of common prayer to hear Divine Service for the space of three weeks 14 July last at St Maughans.[2]

This seems to be the last time that a Catholic was summoned to appear at the Assizes on purely religious grounds in the county of Monmouthshire, although no convictions have been recorded. Robert was later to became a churchwarden of St Maughans and presented the church with a large bell. But he did not inherit the Hilston Estate, as he died in April 1720, three years before his father.

St Meughans' Church, St. Maughans

Robert and his wife Anne, who died one month after him, are buried in the church at St Maughans. In 1753, the estate of Hilston Park was granted to his son, also Robert, after being administered by the grandmother and guardian, Susanna (Susan) Needham, since 1724.[2]

So in the 18th century, the house jumped a generation. Robert and Anne's son became the next owner. He married Elizabeth, daughter of Robert Rowe of Leigh, Somerset. He died in April 1769 and is also buried at St Maughans, she died seven years later at Bath, in Somerset. Their son John, married Lelia,[3] daughter of Thomas Havers of Thelton Hall, in Thelveton, Norfolk.

---

3. Rosa-Lelia according to John Burke's *Genealogical and Heraldic History of the Commoners of Great Britain and Ireland*; Lelia according to Bradney, *Hundred of Skenfrith*

It was probably this John Needham, a barrister with quarters in London's Gray's Inn, who influenced the road layout as we see it today. Before the turnpike road through Newcastle was constructed in the 1780s, the road from Monmouth to Norton and Grosmont was not much more than a track. The new toll road had been completed as far as the Old Boot junction, and was continuing down the original route to The Lade House - a cider house until the 1800s - and then on to Norton. The road to The Lade had already been widened for 500 yards, when the owner of Hilston requested that the road turn right at the Boot corner onto the old Pilgrim Road and continue to Crossways, passing Hilston on the right – this road would then join the old road of Norton to St Maughans at Crossways.

The new road, from the Old Boot to Crossways, had to be built up in two places. Firstly at a spot which is now outside the North Lodge (not then in existence), this part was raised for about 100 yards. Secondly, before the hamlet of Crossways, for another 100 yards above the level of the field. The road consequently gave better access to the north side of the mansion. Up to this time, the main drive to the house on the west side had been across the fields to St Maughans. The smithy, noted on maps before then, was re-sited at Crossways possibly in the 1840s during the time of Robert Brownrigg, who built the Barracks and then improved the access to the north side of Hilston and bypassed the farm buildings. The redundant smithy building may well have been then left to serve as a northern lodge, leaving it to the Grahams, in 1912, to rebuild it to the North Lodge we see today.

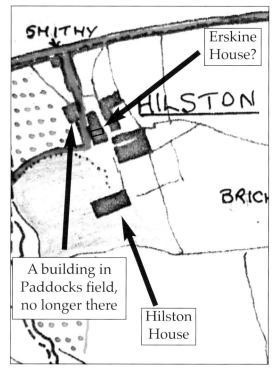

In 1803, John Needham sold Hilston and moved to Somerset. Sebastian Needham and his descendants had owned the estate for well over 100 years, longer than any other family. But in the following century, Hilston changed hands no fewer than ten times.

PEDIGREE OF THE FAMILY OF NEEDHAM

The family crest of arms was;
argent, a bend engrailed azure between
two buck's heads cabossed sable [3]

Sebastian Needham
buried at Skenfrith 20th March 1667
§
Robert Needham [4]
d. March 1723
m. Susan, daughter to Turberville Morgan of Cilgoed, d. 1739
§
Robert Needham [5]
d April 1720, buried at St Maughans
m. firstly Lucy Scudamore
m. secondly Anne, daughter to Edward Pye, The Mynde,[6] d. May 1720
§
Robert Needham
d. April 1769
m. Elizabeth, daughter to Robert Rowe of Somerset
§
John Needham
m. Lelia (Rosa-Lelia) daughter, Thomas Havers, Thelton Hall, Thelveton

During the time Needhams were at Hilston, at least seven members of the family became priests.

An entry in the Perthîr Register for a baptism reads:

John, son of Robert Needham and his wife Elizabeth, was born 19th August 1752, and baptised 23rd August 1752 by the Rev. John Hickins. Godfather, John Vaughan Esqre of Hunstsham, [Huntsham Herefordshire] and Godmother, Mary Roe.

---

3. Joseph Bradney (1904) *Hundred of Skenfrith* page 58
4. A brother to Sebastian (Jesuit Priest), John, Mary, Ursula, Elizabeth
5. Brother to John (Priest, St Francis) and Charles, (Priest)
6. Formerly Saddlebow

The stone in the aisle of the nave at St Maughans Church, (outlined), bears the inscription (now almost illegible): Underneath this stone lies interred the Remains of Robert Needham of Hilston, Esq. who died April y e 17th 1769, Aged 51. Also of Robert and Ann Needham, his father and mother, the first of whom died April y e 11, 1720, the latter May y e 20th, 1720. May they rest in peace.

Pontyrehen Farm, Llanvihangel-Ystern-Llewern, the house built
by Needhams whilst living at Hilston

During their long stay at Hilston, the Needham family built a house at Pont-yr-ychen, meaning Bridge of the Oxen, at what was then called Llannehangell-Eslyrnllowyrn, now Llanvihangel-Ystern-Llewern.

John Erskine, 1694 - 1716

John Erskine, 1694 -1750, was born at Hilston Park on the 6th January, 1694 and is recorded [1] as being a son of Sir John Erskine, the 23rd Earl of Mar, an important Jacobite military leader, and Jane of Newcastle (Monmouthshire).

Sir John Erskine, 23rd Earl of Mar was described in volume five of *Scots Peerage* [2] as 'a man of good sense, but bad morals'. It is not improbable that Sir John had an illegitimate child. Although it is recorded that his son John was born at Hilston, Sir John did not marry his first wife, Lady Margaret Hay, until April 1703 at Twickenham, London. It was Sir John Erskine who raised the standard for a Jacobite rising in September 1715. However, he proved to be no great military leader and lost the battle of Sherriffmuir.

Three months later, the Jacobite rebellion had been quashed, the leaders were impeached and some were executed; estates and titles were forfeited by an Act of Parliament. The earl then promptly fled to exile in France. It was following this that John (of Hilston) - being the son of a Jacobite rebel leader - fled to America in 1716 where he landed at Portsmouth, New Hampshire. It is believed he used the name John Erskine de Mar at first, and then simply John Marr. By 1719 at age 25 he lived in Kittery, Maine. He married Catherine Surplus, only daughter of John and Elizabeth Surplus, on 16th July, 1719. The few records available refer to him as a mariner, and it is possible he made his living in this manner. John was shipwrecked in 1750 at Cape Cod, Barnstable, Massachusetts and died from exposure. He was buried at Frost, near Eliot, Maine.

In the mid 1820s, believing that he was a descendant of the 23rd Earl of Mar, a number of his American descendants were prompted to vie for the title of earldom - which by then had been restored to a nephew of John - and tried to claim the fortunes of the Mar estates in Scotland. Over the next 40 years they spent $50,000 in legal fees, but failed. The birth of John Erskine de Marr - the son of John, Earl of Mar, and Jane of Newcastle - was recorded in the parish records of Llangattock-Vibon-Avel, the church near Hilston

1. James F. Jamison (1985) *The Descendants of John and Catherine Marr of Kittery*
2. Sir James Balfour Paul (1904) *Scots Peerage*

Park, but sometime in the 1840s, during the time of this protracted court case, some of the records for this parish disappeared, including those for his birth year of 1694, so no firm proof of John's lineage was ever established. *Scots Peerage* of 1904 is founded on works of the 18th century and is regarded as being the definitive reference to Scottish nobility. Volume nine, relating to the lineage of Erskine, makes no mention of a son named John, it is only the book of James Jamison that gives rise to this line of descent.

While it is not easy to determine the exact date the family moved into Hilston, there seems to be some possible overlap of occupancy between the Erskine and Needham families. It is quite possible that young John Erskine lived at Hilston with his mother, Jane, at the same time as the Needhams. There were other buildings around Hilston many years ago, apart from the main house, that were used for accommodation. One such building is just off the north drive to the mansion, and used to be a house (page 34). The Needhams, being a Catholic family, would have had some sympathies to the Jacobite cause, which was closely linked to Catholicism. The Compton Census of 1676,[3] showed there to be many Catholic parishes in north Monmouthshire, such as Skenfrith, St Maughans, Llangattock-Vibon-Avel, and Rockfield, all possible well-known gathering places for Jacobite sympathisers.

When Vernon Pugh bought the Home Farm in 1956, he can remember an old house with a large boiler downstairs - now a cattle water trough - a very large stone kitchen sink and a wooden staircase leading to a first floor room with a fireplace. It has now been converted into animal housing, but it was quite obviously used for living accommodation many years ago. Another building - which no longer remains today - was in the Paddocks field, between the main road and Hilston, where there is still a wooden animal shelter, but early maps indicate a much larger building of some kind. Either of these two places may well be where John and his mother lived, while Sir John was away in London, Scotland or abroad.

It is interesting to note that one hundred and fifty years later, in September 1866, John Francis Goodeve-Erskine married Alice Sinclair, the eldest daughter of the late John Hamilton Esquire, of Hilston Park. Also in that year, he was bestowed the title of the 27th Earl of Mar. The Countess of Mar (Alice?) was listed as a vice-president in the 1875 Subscription List of the Bristol and West of England Society for Women's Suffrage.

3. An ecclesiastical census, one of the main sources for estimating population totals in the late 17th century.

William Pilkington 1803 - 1815

In 1753, the Pilkington family bought the Palladian style Chevet Hall, Yorkshire, which incorporated the Country Park at Newmillerdam, and used the 2,340 acre estate for hunting and fishing. They developed a very profitable coal and lead mining industry on the estate in the 1800s; this may explain how William Pilkington made a fortune at such an early age.

In 1803, John Needham sold Hilston to the architect Sir William Pilkington (1775-1850), eighth baronet of Chevet Hall, in Chevin. William was born at Wakefield in 1775, and bought Hilston Park in 1803 at the age of 28. He must have lived there as a bachelor, as he didn't marry until 1825.

William Pilkington was a very successful architect and was commissioned to design many buildings, including a replacement Chilton Lodge in Berkshire, completed around 1800. The building incorporated a four columned full height Corinthian portico, similar to that which now fronts Hilston. Whilst living at Hilston, he was involved in extending Clermont Lodge, Norfolk in 1812, as well as work on Folkestone Gaol, Portsmouth Customs House and many alterations to private homes.

In 1815, the year he left Hilston Park, William Pilkington commissioned the famous landscape painter, Joseph Mallord William Turner,[1] to paint the watercolour, 'On the Washburn, under Folly Hall'. The landscape shows the ruined Dob Hall on the hilltop in the background. Dob Hall was a 17th century hunting lodge on the edge of the Washburn Valley, near Otley. Another scene painted by Turner was of Otley Chevin, a well-known hill in West Yorkshire. The sportsman posing in the foreground of the painting is William Pilkington. Entitled 'Woodcock Shooting on Otley Chevin', it now forms part of the Wallace Collection.

In 1825, ten years after he sold Hilston House, Sir William married Mary Swinnerton, daughter and co-heir to the estate of Thomas Swinnerton and his wife Mary, herself the daughter and heir of the late Charles Milborne of Wonastow, Monmouth and the Priory Estate, Abergavenny. They had

1. Friends through the mutual acquaintance of Walter Fawkes, MP of Farnley Hall, Otley

three sons; the eldest, Edward Pilkington the 9th baronet, died without issue, as did his brother Sir William Pilkington, 10th baronet. They were succeeded by the third brother, Sir Lionel Pilkington, 11th baronet of Chevet, Yorkshire and Wonastow, Monmouthshire, who assumed the surname Milborne-Swinnerton-Pilkington in 1856. He deposited the Milborne family papers and documents with the National Library of Wales.

Chevet Hall, the Pilkington family home in Yorkshire, was sadly demolished in 1955 by Wakefield Council (to much local disapproval) following subsidence caused by the mining of the 1800s. The only parts of the park that remain today are the boathouse, built by William Pilkington in 1820, and some of the nine lodges around the private estate.

The boathouse today in the former park of Chevet Hall built by William Pilkington Picture courtesy Steven Woodcock

'On the Washburn, under Folly Hall'
The painting is on display in the British Museum, reg no 1910,0212.287
Reproduced here by kind permission of the British Museum.

James Jones 1815 - 1821

The next occupant, in 1815, was James Jones of the Graig Estate, Cross Ash, Monmouthshire. He was an attorney in Brecon and had been a resident at Llan Thomas, an ancient mansion in the parish of Llanigon. He was High Sheriff of Brecknockshire in 1810 and was married to Joanna, daughter of Charles Prichard, a surgeon in Brecon and London.

The Graig was an estate at Cross Ash, purchased by James Jones from his brother-in-law William Prichard. Whilst he resided at Hilston, (although it's unclear whether he actually bought the house, or merely rented it) he carried out renovation work at the Graig house and buildings. Hilston Park and the Graig estates shared several boundaries, but after just a few years Jones left Hilston, and Robert Brownrigg took up residence in 1821.

James Jones died in 1836.

Graig House, Cross Ash in 2012, the home of Mrs Colombo

**By Direction of the Administrators of the Estate of the late Herbert Edward Mardon.
Settled by the Will of James Howe Mardon deceased.**

MONMOUTHSHIRE

Forming part of the village of Cross Ash, and in the Parishes of Skenfrith,
Llantilio Crossenny and Grosmont.

Particulars with plans and conditions of Sale of the

FREEHOLD AGRICULTURAL ESTATE

known as

THE GRAIG ESTATE

CROSS ASH

1430·190 Acres (or thereabouts)

comprising

**13 EXCELLENT FARMS, 9 COTTAGES, A FULLY LICENSED ROADSIDE INN
AND SUNDRY PARCELS OF ACCOMMODATION LAND.**

Producing an Annual Rental of £950.

Auctioneers :
Messrs. J. STRAKER, CHADWICK & SONS,
Abergavenny.   Telephone 24/25.
and at Crickhowell and Ewyas Harold.

Land Agent :
OAKDEN FISHER, ESQ.,
(Messrs. Gabb, Price & Fisher),
Solicitors, Abergavenny.
Telephone 14.

Solicitors :
Messrs. CRAWLEY, ARNOLD, ELLIS & ELLIS,
2 & 3, The Sanctuary,
Westminster, London, S.W.1.
Telephone : Abbey 6491.

*The following pages are extracts from the 1954 sale catalogue of The Graig Estate,
139 years after the time of James Jones*

LOT 1

(Coloured   on Plan)

Area subject to Tenancy   ....   **543.501** acres
Area previously in hand   ....   **226.577** acres
                                 ———————
                                 770.078 acres
                                 ———————

Let to Mr. C. A. S. Livesey upon a yearly tenancy

Rent £344–7–0 per annum

THE HEALTHY STOCK RAISING FARMS

known as

THE GRAIG FARMS

which comprise the following holdings :—

CEFN-Y-GRAIG

PART CELYN LANDS

CAE ROBIN

NEW HILL FARM

UPPER GRAIG

LITTLE GRAIG

SUMMARY OF LOTS

Lot No.	Name of Property.	Tenant.	Acreage.
1.	Cefn-y-Graig. Cae Robin. Part Celyn Lands. New Hill Farm, Upper Graig.	C. A. S. Livesey	770.078
2.	Cross Ash Farm	A. W. Jones	222.371
3.	Trebella Farm	G. A. Williams	146.485
4.	The New Inn	T. A. Baylis	52.426
5.	The Stores	F. Nash	18.251
6.	Heald Farm	H. E. Morgan	34.594
7.	Blaen Lymmon	W. A. Price	76.169
8.	The Graig	F. Jones	32.077
9.	The Celyn	Miss Meredith	20.688
10.	The Pugatory	L. J. H. Luntley	25.339
11.	The Dunkard	J. Martin	16.278
12.	1/2, The Fingerpost	A. H. Martin Miss G. M. Thomas	2.469
13.	3, The Fingerpost	Mrs. Curr	.065
14.	4, The Fingerpost (site of Garage)	Mrs. Cornish do.	.340
15.	1, The Old Police Station	Mrs. E. Evans	.432
16.	2, The Old Police Station	J. Williams	.160
17.	Kennel Cottage	O. C. Meredith	.347
18.	Cae Yu	Mr. Cross	.100
19.	The Hall Woodland	In hand	3.321
20.	Dufty's Land	Mr. Dufty	8.300

TOTAL   .... 1430.190 acres.

2

General Robert Brownrigg 1821 - 1833

One of Hilston's most colourful owners, General Sir Robert Brownrigg, 1st baronet GCB - described by Joseph Bradney in his History of Monmouth as 'a distinguished officer in the Peninsula War' - appeared in 1821. Robert Brownrigg was born in Ireland in 1759, and was commissioned as an ensign in 1775. In 1789, he married Elizabeth Catharine Lewis, and they had six sons and a daughter.

In 1795, after good service with the Ninth Foot, Brownrigg was appointed military secretary to the Duke of York, brother of George IV, and accompanied him to the Helder in Holland in 1799. Then, in 1803, he was appointed Quartermaster-General to the Forces, a post he held until 1811, which made him responsible for the supply of equipment, provisions and munitions. It was during this time, in 1804, that his wife Catharine, died. In July 1809, he joined the expedition to the Schelt, and the following year he married Sophia Bissett. In 1813, he was appointed Governor of Ceylon, a position he held until 1820. He conquered the kingdom of Kandy, an independent monarchy in the interior of the island, and with the Kandyan Convention of 1815 unified the island under British rule. He was created a baronet in 1816, and attained the full rank of General in 1818. There was a major rebellion in Ceylon in 1817, known as the Uva Rebellion or the Third Kandyan War, which was suppressed in very bloody fashion.

Brownrigg retired to Hilston in 1821 paying 22,000 guineas for the estate. The old soldier took a keen interest in the welfare of the local community, and offered Crossways field as the site for a new school for Skenfrith and Llangattock-Vibon-Avel. But owing to the distances some children would have to walk, the idea was later abandoned.

General Sir Robert Brownrigg, GCB
Picture courtesy of the British Museum

Brownrigg died at Hilston in 1833, aged 74, his wife Sophia died four years later. *The Merlin* reported on the 8th June, 1833, that his funeral was attended by 'about 200 relatives, friends and tradesmen'.

Among the items sold at Hilston after his death - probably brought back from Ceylon - were a 'magnificent bookcase of calamander wood, cabinets filled with stuffed Indian birds, shells and numerous Cingalese books'. It is reported that he had brought over large quantities of calamander wood

and some of the additions he made to Hilston included constructing the doors to the dining room out of this highly polished wood.

During his time in Ceylon, Brownrigg also acquired an impressive gilded bronze stature of the Buddhist goddess Tara, which he donated to the British Museum in 1830.

It is currently on display in their Asia department, this photograph and more details can be seen on the museum's web site, www.britishmuseum.org.

The statue of the Goddess Tara, donated to the British Museum by Brownrigg is on display in the Asia Dept, room 33.

Ref; Asia OA 1830.6-12.4

Height 143 cm
Width, 44cm
Depth 29.5cm

In the Radio 4 programme *A History of the World in 100 Objects*, the statue was item no. 54

**Picture reproduced courtesy of
The British Museum**

The school planned for Crossways

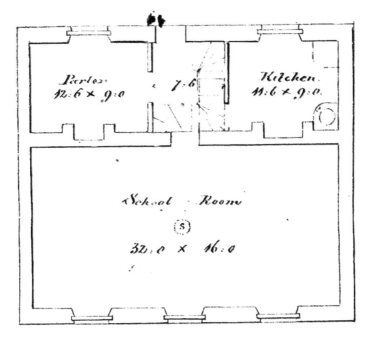

These drawings are reproduced from the Jack Axten Collection

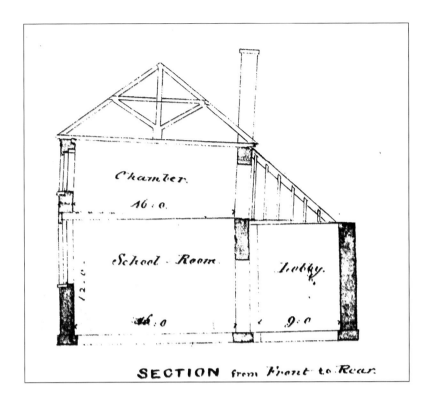

SECTION from Front to Rear.

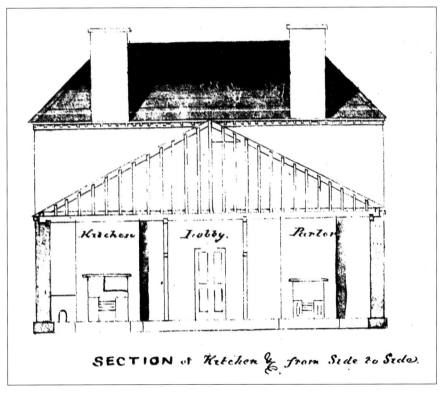

SECTION of Kitchen &c. from Side to Side.

Norton Cross was chosen as the new site for a school for the Skenfrith area. In 1826, Brownrigg founded the first school for the Llangattock and Newcastle area, situated at Newcastle (in the parish of Llangattock-Vibon-Avel), in the building which was until recently the Post Office and stores, and is now appropriately named The Old Schoolhouse, pictured below.

The Old School House at Newcastle, Monmouthshire,
formerly a shop and Post Office, now a private residence

The School Rules - 1826
Children of the poor inhabitants of the three parishes (Llangattock, St Maughans and Skenfrith) and of such poor parishioners belonging to the parishes as may be resident elsewhere within a convenient distance of the school be admitted in the following manner:
- Each annual subscriber of 10/- shall be at liberty to recommend one poor child and pro rata but all children to be approved by the Committee.
- The Committee shall be at liberty to elect any or all of such children as are not provided for by individual subscribers.
- Children shall assemble from 25th March to 29th September at 9am till 12 noon and 1pm till 4pm and from 29th September they leave at 3pm.
- All children to be sent to school with their hands and faces well washed and their hair well combed - It is expected that the children educated at the National School do attend their respective parish churches each Sunday.

The following account of Newcastle School is taken from the collection of Jack Axten:

Its story is one of mixed fortunes; of periods of wise management and of no management at all; of public generosity and of insolvency; of intense local concern and of apathy. Educational results varied greatly as did the quality of the Master and Mistress, but for more than fifty years it provided the only form of schooling available for the children of the district.

Its end came in 1877 when government intervention in the field of education set up standards with which it could not comply, and its functions were taken over by the Llangattock School, still operating and still in the original building.

What is particularly interesting about the Newcastle School and other similar schools of that time, is that because it was locally managed, almost every local resident comes into its story; from the farmers who hauled the stone for its building, to the Rolls of Hendre who rescued it from extinction, while the names of the Duke of Beaufort and the Bishop appear as its supporters. General Sir Robert Brownrigg bart, G.C.B., had retired to Hilston House in the parish of St. Maughans in or around 1820 after a distinguished career in the army. In 1835, his widow, Lady Sophia Brownrigg, wrote of;

> there never having been any schools of any assistance to the education of the poor children of the surrounding parishes till we went to Hilston

perhaps suggesting that it was realisation of this that induced Sir Robert to take steps to set up a school. It is significant that the children were to come from Llangattock, St. Maughans and Skenfrith; Hilston house stands close to where the three parishes meet.

We are fortunate that there exists in the Local History Centre, Monmouth, the original minute book of the school committee, and also that there are a later minute book and many other papers concerning the school in the Rolls Collection of documents in the County Record Office. The first minute dated 21st January 1825, records a meeting at Hilston House, chaired by Sir Robert Brownrigg, at which were present the vicar and curate of Llangattock, John Norton Esq. of Skenfrith and William Evans, a churchwarden of Llangattock. It was;

> held for the purpose of considering the circumstances connected with the building of a National School at Newcastle in the parish of Llangattock-Vibon-Avel for the education of the children of the parishes of Llangattock, St. Maughans and Skenfrith.

A good deal of progress had already been made by this time. The National Society had voted £120 towards the construction of the building and a total of £204.2s.6d had been raised, £74.2s.6d from subscriptions from the three parishes and £10 from Rev. Norris. The names of 52 donators are mentioned including Sir Robert Brownrigg, £60, Mr Mitchell for £2.3s.6d and William Evans £1.

Mr. Thomas Lawrence (the mason) was engaged for the construction of the building. He submitted an estimate of £235, increased to £248 when it was decided that the roof should be stone tiled. This was considered too high, observing that the operation of hauling materials would be performed by voluntary assistance.

The final figure of £224 was agreed between Sir Robert Brownrigg of Hilston and others and Thomas Lawrence. The dwelling house and school on the green at Newcastle was to be completed by the 1st August 1825. The neighbouring farmers agreed to haul all material, the building agreement refers to it as 'on the green at Newcastle'.

The Reverend John Harding wrote that the school was built on a piece of wasteland, of which there is no regular conveyance because the title was never ascertained, but Mr Rolls had received rent for it for a sufficient number of years to give him - in the opinion of Mr Powles of Monmouth - some sort of title to it.

It was agreed that Richard Cook and his wife Susanna would be appointed master and mistress of the school, with a salary for the two of £20/year. Notice was given in the parish churches that the school would open on Monday 17th July 1826 at 10am. For the first seven years of its existence, the management of the School was watched over by Sir Robert Brownrigg. Subscriptions helped to keep the school running; donations for the year ending June 1834 included £5 from Sir Robert, and £4 from Lady Brownrigg. By September the number of pupils was 79. The last entry in the original minute book reads;

> since the last meeting the committee had to notice with deep regret of Sir Robert Brownrigg [death] - a sincere enact benefactor and truly good man.

Because of Sir Robert's death, the school lost its inspiration and support. It was recorded that King George IV said, 'Sir Robert Brownrigg was one of the best men I ever knew'.[1]

1. *The Merlin*, Saturday 1st June, 1833

Portraits of British Governors of Sri Lanka between 1805 and 1831 were unveiled at Mount Lavinia Hotel Sri Lanka, on 14th July, 2006, - Lt. Gen. Edward Barnes (1819-1821 and 1824-1831), Gov. Edward Paget (1822-1823), Lady Sophia Brownrigg, Gen. Sir Robert Brownrigg (1812-1820) and Sir Thomas Maitland (1805-1811).

Henry Brownrigg, a direct descendant of Sir Robert Brownrigg, unveiled the portrait of his ancestor in 2006, explaining how General Brownrigg had risen through army ranks purely on his own abilities; not easy when commissions had to be purchased. He added that Robert Brownrigg was born in Southern Dublin in the County of Wicklow in 1759 and was gazetted an ensign of the 14th Regiment. He was appointed Governor of Ceylon in 1811, serving there from 1812 until 1820 when he returned to the U.K.

The arms of Brownrigg

He bought Hilston Park the following year.

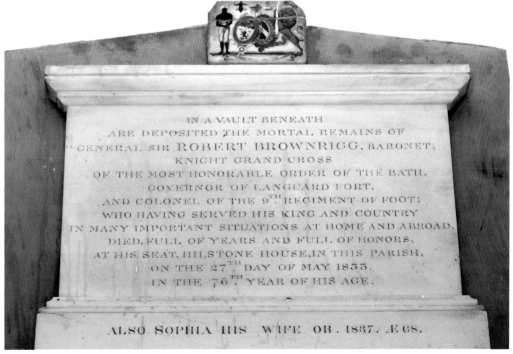

A memorial to the general, together with a plaque showing his coat of arms, can be seen near the south door of St Maughans church. Brownrigg was given special permission to display the arms of the King of Kandy, which can be seen at the top of the memorial together with his own. He is buried in the south wall of St Maughans

Coates and the Great Fire 1833 - 1838

Messrs Burton and Son advertised the sale of 'Hillstone House' on 29th June, 1833 as including '13 cows, 2 oxen, 8 steers, carthorses, pigs and sheep, waggons, ploughs etc and 2,000 gallons of cider. Enquiries Mr Norton, Solicitor, Monmouth'. Hilston was bought in 1833 by Thomas Coates, a Lancashire man who promptly began repairs to the house. In September 1836 as repairs to the roof were in progress, a fire broke out. The following report from *The Merlin*, forerunner of the *Monmouthshire Beacon* of 17th September 1836 is lengthy, but gives a good idea of the atmosphere on the day.

> On Monday afternoon (12th September) about two o'clock a servant reached the town of Monmouth; the alarm bell was tolled, and excitement pervaded the place. The engines were promptly brought forward, and but a very few moments elapsed before they were whirled along at a galloping pace by six horses; on the way one of the engines was impeded by the loss of a linchpin and the breaking of a trace, but it was soon on its journey again…
>
> [When they arrived], it was evident that the roof would soon give way, and immediately on their arrival it fell, a burning wreck, on the ceilings. The fire originated on the roof, in consequence of the reprehensible conduct of blundering stupidity of the person who superintended the plumbing work (the house having been for some time under repair) in allowing his men to make a fire on the top for the purpose of completing some work although he had been refused permission to do so, in the morning, in consequence of the high wind; but this was not the only imprudence; the fire was left while the men went to their dinner and there being at the time a strong north-east wind, it is supposed that some of the embers were blown on the roof, and communicated with the woodwork beneath. The timber of which the roof was composed, as well as the wide cornice under it, was Red Deal, [another name for the softwood, Scot's Pine] which is peculiarly flammable and soon spread the fire round the extent of the building, melting the lead with which it was surrounded and which poured down the house as a dense shower until exhausted, hence the terrific

progress of the devouring element before the engines were brought to act…[A] line was formed for the purpose of conveying water in buckets from the pond on the premises but on account of its distance there was not so abundant supply as could be wished…

[The] furniture upstairs was destroyed… help to save property from lower rooms was most actively and successfully availed of and even many of the window frames were removed; the fine paintings, almost uninjured, and the furniture were placed on the lawn. Some of the marble chimney pieces were also preserved as well as much of the handsome gilt cornices by which the rooms were ornamented; in time almost everything removable was saved from the lower rooms. Meanwhile, nothing could repress the devastating effects of the flames. After the roof had fallen in, the servants' offices with the bedrooms, servants' hall, butler's pantry etc were quickly consumed; the dining room and library shared the same fate in succession leaving but the octagon room and wine cellar to feed the fire. Mr Coates was most anxious to save the octagon… but the beautiful apartment shared the fate of the rest, and the wine cellars (previously emptied) were dilapidated. Mr Coates remained on the spot until near midnight…The engine was left at work occasionally during the night as well as on the succeeding day on the smouldering ruins. Monmouth police were in attendance, some trifling thefts and account of losses were greatly exaggerated. The fire was discovered by a nurse, the only members of the family at home were Miss Coates and Mr Heale. Messengers were sent to Brynderrie, seat of Mr Gisborne, son-in-law to Mr Coates. Mrs Glendinning who with her husband had arrived at Hilston the night before, lost her valuable wardrobe and Mr G's gold chain - valued at 40 guineas - was destroyed. The furniture was insured and the house, it is believed for £2,000. Had the fire not taken place the repairs in progress would have been completed in a fortnight… Mr Coates intends to erect another mansion at Hilston.

Whether through dismay at the loss of his house or for some other reason,* Thomas Coates did not build another mansion at Hilston, but instead sold the estate two years later. There are still charred timbers to be seen in the building .

*Some other reason may be a second fire two years later in 1938. William Graham, writing in 1959/60 spoke of two fires. He claims that 'while the builders were reconstructing the house, another fire occurred and burnt it down again'. His grandfather, James Graham had bought Hilston Park in 1861 (see page 68).

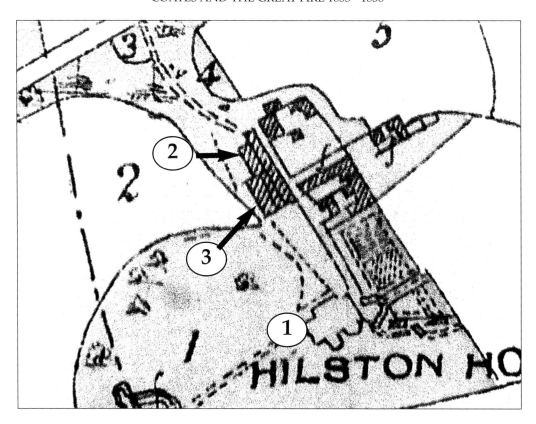

The above map of the estate, from the 1843 tithe map, is interesting as it shows the main house (1) as an unshaded area - was this because the building was still a shell following the fire? The drawing also shows a large cluster of buildings, centre, showing the position of the stable block (2) and the Barracks (3), see page 100

Right and opposite; pictures of the cellar, the only original part of the old building left after the fire and various alterations

Above left, looking down into the old well which still contains some water and above, looking up the well shaft from the cellar. Left; a passageway.
Below, an old part of the cellar, now a storeroom

George Cave 1838 - 1859

Following the fire of 1836, Mr. Thomas Coates had intended to rebuild the Hilston mansion, living meanwhile in The Barracks (see page 102). It was two years before he decided to sell. The sale on the 17th August 1838 (page 103) was not successful; the estate was bought in for 11,000 guineas by the agent George Robins, independent of timber. Brownrigg had given 22,000 guineas for the estate with timber in 1921. *The Merlin* reported on 22nd September 1838 (page 3) that 'within a week of Mr Robins buying Hilston, one of his 'auditory' gave him 2,000 guineas to relinquish his contract'.

In 1838, a Bristol banker called George Cave became Hilston's next owner. Cave was born in 1798, the third son of Stephen Cave, of Cleve Hill, Gloucester and Anne, daughter of Thomas Daniel Esq. of Barbados. He married Anne Halliday in 1820. He was a deputy lieutenant and a JP for Gloucestershire and Devonshire. George Cave was responsible for building much of the classic mansion house that stands today. He also planted a large number of trees, and was responsible for creating the wooded park of nearly 500 acres that gave Hilston its present name; the estate was then called Hilston Park. It is possible that the lake was also [re-?] built to its present day dimensions (see page 132). Bradney,[1] in 1904, considered that 'the plantations around the house… are now just coming to their prime', - but they were all cut down later in 1947 for financial gain.

There are records of a J H Cave, who fought in the Crimea as a lieutenant in the Monmouth Militia, also living at Hilston.[2] In December 1859, in the parish of Frenchay, Gloucestershire, Edward Cave age 30, bachelor Esquire of St Maughans, Monmouth, son of George Cave Esquire, married Susan Harriet Harford age 25, a spinster of Frenchay, daughter of Henry Charles Harford Esquire, witnessed by Henry Charles Harford, George Cave & S H Harford, Captain 12th [Lancers?]. They were married by the Rev. J B Allens. A tower that stands above White House Farm, sometimes referred to as a folly, was almost certainly repaired and improved by Cave. George Cave died on 15th April 1877 at age 79 and is buried in Brompton Cemetery, London.

1. J H Bradney (1904) *Hundred of Skenfrith*
2. *Monmouthshire Beacon* of 31/3/1855 and 29/9/1859

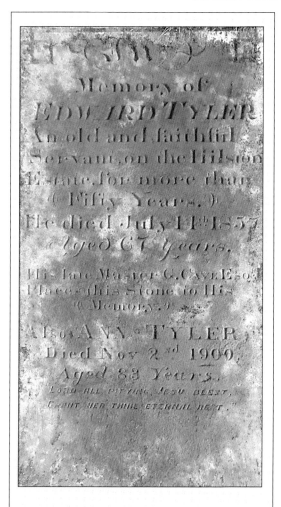

A gravestone in St Maughans churchyard, placed there by George Cave, is in memory of Edward Tyler 'an old and faithful servant on the Hilston Estate of more than 50 years' who died in 1857 and is buried with his wife Anne.

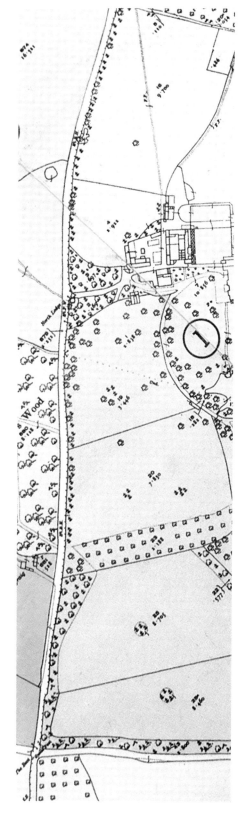

This map from the 1947 sale catalogue shows the tree lined route from Crossways to the Old Boot, planted by Cave.
The line of trees were cut down in 1948

The Crawshay family 1859 - 1861

The Crawshay family were great industrialists; owning the Cyfarthfa Works,[1] northwest of Merthyr Tydfil, from 1794; the Hirwaun Ironworks (operated 1817-1850s) and the Forest Iron Company. In 1879, the Cyfarthfa works was converted to a steel production plant by William Thompson Crawshay, who managed the plant with his son William II. Cyfarthfa closed in 1921. The family's main seat was at Cyfarthfa Castle, but it also bought estates at Hilston Park and Caversham Park.

Around 1859, William Crawshay purchased Hilston from George Cave, but it was his son-in-law/nephew, Alfred, who is recorded as resident at this time, (a possible wedding gift from William to his daughter and son-in-law?). A valuation of the live and dead stock, including hay, straw, manure and 'tillaged' on the Home Farm, dated 5th April, 1860, is currently kept at the National Library of Wales in the Crawshay Archives. Two pages record that the valuation, from George Cave to William Crawshay, was £737.15s.0d.

Alfred, a captain in the 17th Lancers, married his cousin, Jessy Crawshay, the daughter of his uncle, William Crawshay, and aunt Isobel (née Thompson, William's second wife). Alfred was a son of George Crawshay, a brother to the William that bought Hilston Park. Alfred and Jessy had five children; Alfred, Codrington, (who was a JP and deputy lieutenant for the county of Monmouth), Isabel, Willoughby and Jessy. After only a short while, William Crawshay sold the estate to John Hamilton.

Alfred died in 1864 in London aged 41 and Jessy died in 1889. She is recorded in the 1881 census as widowed and living at Dan y Park aged 60. Dan y Park is a mansion on the banks of the river Usk. There is a memorial to Alfred and Jessy Crawshay in the south cemetery of Llanelly Parish Church, Monmouthshire. It is a listed CADW monument, building ID 23803, (see opposite).

1. In 1765, Anthony Bacon established, in partnership with William Brownrigg, the Cyfarthfa Furnace. The outbreak of the American Civil War enabled them to develop the casting of guns already established at Cyfarthfa and extend operations by leasing two furnaces; The Plymouth Furnace at Merthyr Tydfil in 1777 and the Hirwaun Furnace in 1780

The memorial to Alfred, Jessy and Psyche in Llanelly Parish Church cemetery

The inscriptions read:

Alfred Crawshay Esq.
of Dan y Park.
late Captain in the
17th Lancers.
Died in London
April 26th 1864
in his 41st year.
Not lost but gone
before

In loving memory of
my mother
Jessy Crawshay,
July 17th 1889.
There the wicked cease
from troubling and there the
weary are at rest

A third inscription
reads:

Our little darling
Psyche
died June 26 1889
11 months old
Only an angel sent to
shew me the way
to heaven

Psyche was a grand-
daughter to Jessy and the
Late Alfred Crawshay
and the daughter of
Jessy, who married
Robert Preston in 1884
at Crickhowell

Alfred and Jessy Crawshay had been tenants at Llwynwormwood, in the parish of Myddfai, Llandovery. It is a former coach house to the now ruined 13 bedroom country house that stood nearby. It is this house that was bought by Prince Charles in 2006 as a base for his visits to Wales and has been converted into a three bedroom farmhouse.

John Hamilton 1861 - 1873

John Hamilton the younger of Liverpool, was born on 25th January 1818. He bought Hilston in 1861, in his deeds the house was referred to as Upper Hilston and Hilston Park. John Hamilton completed the building to what it was before the fire, and added the large pillars at the front of the house. He had a considerable fortune and planned to make Hilston into a large estate. In 1861, according to the deeds, the estates consisted of the Mansion and Demesne Farm (Home Farm) referred to as Llanlyke. Other farms on the estate were:

Llanlikey Ycha now Upper Grove; Hill Farm now called White House Farm, Crossways; the cottage adjoining called Goodmans with two acres; Lower Hilston containing 107 acres; Tyn Gaut (Tre Gout), 95 acres with land in Skenfrith and adjoining land with Norton Court, (315 acres).

Plas Ivor Farm, Cross Ash, neighbour to Lyvos

In October 1862, Hamilton purchased Plas Ivor (228 acres), Lyvos (204 acres) and four other pieces of pasture and woodland from the Duke of Beaufort, Messrs Sir H A and P R Hoare and Edward Tylee, and added the following farms to the estate:

Rhulin and Coedangro, [Ruthlin and Coed Anghred], Ricketts [Quarry Farm], Woodside and St. Freada [St Fraeds].

From Thomas Davies of Nevadd, Brecon the following:

Duffryn, Box Farm, Pant, [opposite White House Farm, one mile from Norton on the Grosmont road], Trevoney, Birch Hill and New House or Upper House Farm; altogether 942 acres.

He also added:

Upper and Lower Clappers, Tump Farm and Norton Cottage.[1]

1. From the Deeds of the Home Farm

Also purchased in 1865, from Marta Embry of Garway and Thomas Nicholas of Orcop, was the King's Head and garden at Newcastle, Llangattock-Vibon-Avel. This property is situated opposite the old Post Office and shop, (page 50) - it has been known as Hillside, Christmas Cottage and now Bryn-y-Felin. On an estate map of 1804, it was marked as Hilstone Arms, possibly a cider house in Needham and Pilkington's time. Hamilton had enlarged the Hilston Estate by buying Norton Court Farm (6th May, 1862) from the eighth Duke of Beaufort, as well as Lower Duffryn and Skenfrith Mill. He died on the 20th December 1868, two years before his mother,

The King's Head

Mary. He is buried in the Hamilton family vault, on the north side of St. Maughans Church, overlooking Hilston. John Hamilton's will of February 1868 appointed his wife Ann (née Jones, daughter of Pryce Jones, of Cysfronydd, Montgomeryshire) and David Jones, his brother-in-law, to be executors and trustees. The estate was in trust during the lifetimes of his wife, Ann Hamilton, and their son Captain Pryce Hamilton and after to any sons of Pryce. The estate did pass to his son Captain Pryce Hamilton – although the latter may never have actually lived here. Pryce Bowman Hamilton was born in 1844, the only son of John Hamilton of Hilston Park, and Anne Jones. He had three sisters :

- Alice Mary Sinclair; the eldest daughter, who married the Rev. John Francis Goodeve-Erskine 27th Earl of Mar.

- Laura Jane Campbell; born 7th Feb 1850 at Hilston Park, died 9th May 1922, who married Lt.-Col. Henry Charles Eden Malet, Bt.

- Mary Elizabeth Hamilton who married Captain Pennant Lloyd of Bangor.[2]

Pryce Bowman Hamilton
Picture courtesy Djedj Lantz

2. Montgomeryshire Collections, Volume 19 pp 142.3

In the deeds of November 1873, Ann Hamilton and David Jones exercised their power with consent of Pryce Bowman Hamilton, (her son), to sell the estate to James Graham for the sum of £119,000, the whole of the estate measuring 2,830 acres. Pryce Hamilton went to live at Wilton near Ross-on-Wye, Herefordshire.

The grave and crypt of John Hamilton at the north side of
St Maughans Church, looking towards Hilston Park

The Hilston Estate was advertised for sale in 1873 in The Times

Hilston Estate advertised in The Times in 1873 by Captain Pryce Hamilton, sold to James Graham

A most attractive and valuable Freehold Domain of nearly 3,000 acres, picturesquely situate and distinguished as the Hilston Estate, in the parishes of Llangattock, St Maughan's, Skenfrith, Grosmont and Llandillio Cresseny, six miles from Monmouth, county of Monmouth [sic]. Within its own surrounding and spacious park is Hilston-house, a handsome and most commanding moderate size building of stone and brick, in the Palladian style, commanding the most extensive and varied views of a well wooded country - stretching on the east from the Malvern Range in Worcestershire to the more rugged scenery of the mountains of Wales on the west.

The reception rooms are of a most elegant design, comprising dining room 30ft. by 21ft., large drawing room 30ft. by 22ft., and a smaller one 18ft. 6in by 15ft., communicating with each other, and with the conservatory 37ft. in length, library 25ft. by 15ft 6in, study and cloak room. There are nine large and four small sleeping apartments.

Another building offers extra accommodation for the reception of bachelor guests, having 13 bedrooms and a large billiard room or dining room.

The domestic offices are everything that could be desired. The stabling which is complete as it possibly could be, consists of eight large loose boxes and six stalls and coach-house for five or six carriages.

The farm buildings are most substantial and ample. The gardens are inexpensive to keep up and are in first rate order. The park is 400 acres in extent on which is timber of a most promising character. The estate is in every respect most compact, and is divided into 15 farms, with capital outbuildings.

The actual and estimated income of the whole is £2,933 per annum, presenting an opportunity of purchasing a fine landed estate which is an investment and as a residential property in every way desirable.

The Graham family 1873 - 1918

On 28th November 1873, a magistrate called James Graham bought Hilston Park for the sum of £119,000. On 22nd June 1874, he enlarged it with the purchase of Carters Farm, at the cost of £990. The estate extended into the parishes of St Maughans, Llangattock-Vibon-Avel, Skenfrith, Grosmont and Rockfield,[1] and its total area was approximately 3,000 acres. By 1905, the Grahams also owned The Bell Inn at Skenfrith, it was referred to as The Old Bell, and the licensee was Joseph Stepston.

James Graham
James became deputy lieutenant and high sheriff of Monmouthshire in 1881. In 1862 he had married Emily Sophia, the third daughter of the late Henry Robert Kingscote, Esq. They had one son, Douglas William, whom he gave Hilston to in 1903, on the occasion of his son's second marriage. Emily died in 1889, James Graham died in 1908.

Douglas Graham
Major Douglas William Graham was born in 1866. He was educated at Eton, and called to the Bar at the Inner Temple 1895. Formerly a Lieutenant in the Royal Highlanders, and subsequently a Major in the 2nd Battalion, Monmouthshire Regiment, he was also a magistrate and JP for Monmouthshire. In 1889, Douglas married Mary Emmeline, eldest daughter of Major J O Carnegy of Ashbourne Lodge, Abergavenny who died in 1901; they had two sons, William James and Douglas Kingscote. His second marriage, on 11th January 1902, was to Frances Joanna Maud, second daughter of the Rev. William Pinney, formerly rector of Llanvetherine and Caroline Mary (née Pickering), of Blackdown, Dorsetshire. As Douglas and Frances were married at Llanvetherine, it is likely that the Rev. Pinney conducted the marriage. They had two daughters, Joan and Mary Sophia. Rev. Pinney and his wife Caroline both died at Hilston Park; he was 75 and died in 1903, she was 72 and died there in 1904.

---

1. Rockfield Parish, at this time, extended to include the Tump Farm (45 acres), Woodside (133 acres) Rhullin a paper mill (90 acres), Orchard Cottage, and part of Coed Angred. It was not until the boundary changes of 1903 that these farms and cottage were transferred to the parish of Skenfrith.

In a letter sent to Eileen Pritchard, of Park Cottage, Crossways, and given to the author of this book, William Graham, Douglas's son from his first marriage quotes:

> It was probably about 1899 that I first visited Hilston, there were no bathrooms or electric light. The water came from the well beneath the house. My father panelled the hall with panelling taken from Lower Duffryn - the panelling up the stairs is not old but put in to match. The mahogany [calamander?] doors were in the original house long before our time, when the fires[2] took place, they were taken off their hinges and put on the lawn, hence their existence today. My father added the two front windows in the entrance hall. The new wing including the large room at the end of the veranda (which we called the Oak Parlour) was built by my father (Douglas) in 1911. We used the lake for fishing, catching some trout and coarse fish.

Douglas was clearly an energetic character, and he made many changes to the estate. He panelled the fine hall, pictured below, with oak he had removed from the hall of Lower Duffryn; the farm on the right hand side of the Grosmont road, two miles from the Norton crossroads.

The main hall to Hilston, with panelling from the Lower Duffryn

2. It is possible that the repairs being carried out to the roof, following the first fire, caused a second fire in 1938, giving some truth to the references of two fires.

Joseph Bradney [3] was of the opinion that 'Mr Graham, (pictured inset [4]), has much improved the interior of the house by panelling the hall'.

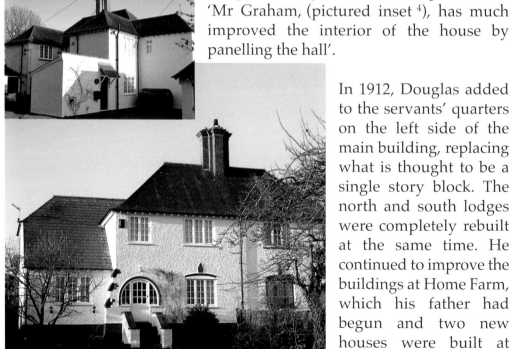

In 1912, Douglas added to the servants' quarters on the left side of the main building, replacing what is thought to be a single story block. The north and south lodges were completely rebuilt at the same time. He continued to improve the buildings at Home Farm, which his father had begun and two new houses were built at Crossways, pictured left.

3. Bradney (1904) *Hundred of Skenfrith*, page 58
4. Picture of Douglas Graham courtesy of the Graham family

The former servants' quarters from the front. Later the first floor was used as a flat for residential staff, now converted to extra accommodation for outdoor pursuit activities Below; an early shot from the back, shows the house before the servants' quarters were extended upwards on the right hand side of the building

Writing on the back of the postcard above, Mrs Graham says:
The single window at the left is the day nursery, next to that is the Blue Room. The next bay window Mr G's room. Under the day nursery, the Boudoir; under the Blue, the drawing room; under Mr G's room, the dining room. The lake is just at the end of this lawn down the front and the summer house at the right end down the steps. When it is wet, the children play under the colonade.

He also built the reservoir at Cae Graig, which replaced the old system whereby water from the well beneath the house was pumped to tanks at the top of Hilston House. The supply was connected to the estate farms and houses in 1916 and pumped from a spring in the field opposite the North Lodge. The reservoir was on the land of the Black-brooke Estate, owned by the

The pumphouse containing the spring

Newton-Jackson family, and when that land was sold in 1920, it was stipulated that the reservoir and water supply pipes from there to Hilston must be maintained, along with the right of entry to inspect, repair or renew the reservoir or pipes in the event of damage. The supply was disconnected by Monmouthshire County Council in the early 1990s; water is now supplied by the mains.

Douglas Graham left Hilston in 1918, but was invited back to Skenfrith to lead the parade from the church to the newly erected war memorial in 1920. In that year, Douglas Graham bought Brynderwen Court, near Bettws Newydd, He sold it in 1930 and bought Wonastow Court in the parish of Wonastow, Monmouthshire.[5]

In his letter, William Graham continues:

> During my time at Hilston my father's father-in-law, the Rev. Pinney from Llanvetherine and his wife, on his retirement, came to live at The Barracks. After the death of the Rev. Pinney, his wife went to live at the Rectory at Llanvetherine, now called The Meadows, situated by the Church.

William also commented on the first house after Crossways on the left-hand side of the road leading to Linthill - which was then known as the Cottage Hospital - and is now called Caldy House, pictured opposite. 'I believe a small cottage hospital was built for my grandmother, which she supervised until her death in 1889'. *William Graham 1960.*

5. This information came from Mr Peter Graham, 'The Tors', Whitwell Road, Ventnor, Isle of Wight, who visited Hilston Park in the 1990s

The hospital at Crossways was built in the late 1870s and closed around 1903, when a hospital was opened in Monmouth on the Hereford Road. The Cottage Hospital with about three acres of land was then let to a butcher called Thomas Oriel, and in 1921, when Mrs Lawley sold the estate (page 76), he bought it. He and his wife Alice were still living there in 1935, but the latter subsequently sold the property to Ernie Parry.

Roley Price (Tre Gout) recalled that Douglas Graham had a car that he (Douglas) drove to London on a regular basis. The last part of the return journey was made with the assistance of horses; waggoners from Hilston would take their horses down to Norton crossroads to meet the car and tow it back to the house via Crossways. The Graham family would often travel to Llangattock Church by Brougham along the drive to South Lodge.

Members of the Graham family still retain an interest in their old family home. In the 1960s, Clive Graham, a member of the Grahams of Hilston, called in to see his ancestral home. He had been for many years, the racing correspondent for the Daily Express, writing under the pseudonym of 'The Scout'. Another family member, William Graham, is currently the Conservative AM for southeast Wales, a member of the Welsh Government. Isobel Veldekens, née Graham, came to the Home Farm in the 1990s to visit Hilston Park, her great-grandfather's home. She now lives in Belgium.

Caldy House, Crossways

The Lawley family 1918 - 1921

In 1918, the Hilston Estate was bought by Arthur Ernest Lawley after he had put in an offer for the estate following a shooting expedition there when the house and estate took his eye. In late 1919 he purchased the neighbouring Garway estate of 2,751 acres for £37,550, and promptly put the majority of that estate back on the market - with John D Wood and Co, London - on 14th January 1920, retaining the Lordship of the Manor of Garway and the fishing rights on the river Monnow. Not all of the 61 lots were sold, Glanmonnow (Glenmonnow) House being one of them.

Arthur Lawley did not live at Hilston long, as he died on 26 May 1920, aged 45. The report in the *Monmouthshire Beacon* two days later said:

> The deceased was a keen angler. In fact it was only on Thursday of last week that he caught a chill while fishing, and this set up the illness which resulted fatally, despite the best of medical attention. He leaves a widow and two daughters.

A memorial service was held in St Maughans Church, Mr Lawley's coffin having been carried in relays by his employees across the fields to the church. The address was given by Rev. C E de la Billière, who described Lawley as 'a supremely genial, generous and able reviver of life on [the] land', and said that he 'had become the fount and centre of new industrial and social life and energy, and of happiness and prosperity to a rustic community'.

Arthur Lawley was buried in Alderley Edge, Cheshire, his ancestral home.

Right; Arthur Lawley's grave in Alderley Edge

The cause of death, as certified by A L Fatham MB on his death certificate was pneumonia.

The Hereford Times reported in 1920 that he died intestate, leaving estate to the gross value of £360,000 but it is interesting to note that a conveyance dated 7th February 1921, between Elizabeth Lawley, and Artis Alfred Ruck of Garway makes reference to a will made by Arthur Lawley in 1905, when he had appointed as executors and trustees his father, Arthur Lawley and Frederick Plews. But three years after the will was made, his father died and Frederick Plews rendered probate alone.

Elizabeth Lawley had no need for Hilston Park Estate and its 3,372 acres, which included the unsold Glanmonnow House, and put the whole estate up for sale on May 19th 1921, again with John D Wood and Co. The Hilston Estate was described in the catalogue as;

> one of the finest domains in this glorious country, comprising 3,371 acres of beautifully disposed, wood-capped hills and broad vales with six miles of trout fishing on the River Monnow and unrivalled shooting.

Lot one was the mansion, with nearly three miles of fishing and 1,771 acres; lot two was Glenmonnow House (now Glanmonnow) with 1,130 acres and fishing; lot three was Lower Duffryn Farm with 469 acres and fishing. The main house was described as having '20 bed and dressing rooms, five bathrooms, five reception rooms, panelled halls, electric light, central heating, telephone, a most comfortable home, economical to run, with splendid model cottages, lodges, home farm and a richly wooded park of 475 acres'. Also up for sale, 'all in good order and let to a good tenantry on short tenancies', were 21 farms.

THE HOME FARM
of 229 Acres

is in hand and carries a pedigree herd of Hereford cattle. The Premises are substantially built of stone, recently thoroughly done up, and afford the following accommodation: Five-stall Cart Stable and Loft, Cow Houses for 17, Bull Box, Chaff Cutting Room, Tractor and Threshing Machine House, Two Hay Barns, Implement Shed, Corn Barn, Granary, Bullock Sheds, Enclosed Yards, etc. In the Park is a Range of Three Bull Boxes with enclosed cemented runs. Water is laid on.

About 45 acres are Arable and the remainder Parkland. Whitehouse Farm of about 183 acres is in hand.

About 2 miles from the Mansion is a comfortable

Dower House

Borders of

Hereford & Monmouth

BETWEEN

THE SALMON RIVERS WYE AND USK

11 *miles from Ross-on-Wye*, 6 *miles from Monmouth (G.W. Rly.)*, 8 *miles from Pontrilas Station (Hereford to Newport)*, 16 *miles from Hereford*.

AS A WHOLE OR IN FOUR LOTS.

The Beautiful

Residential, Sporting and Agricultural Freehold Estate

Hilston Park

comprising

THE FINE MANSION

in perfect order.

A SMALLER RESIDENCE

Exclusive Trout Fishing

in the River Monnow for a distance of about

SIX MILES, MOSTLY BOTH BANKS.

Exceptionally Fine Shooting

including 575 ACRES OF HILLY COVERTS

21 FARMS

3,371 Acres

For Sale by Auction by Messrs.

JOHN D. WOOD & Co.

At Winchester House, Old Broad Street, E.C. (Room 47), on THURSDAY, MAY 19th, at 2.30 p.m., unless previously sold.

Solicitors: Messrs. BOOTE, EDGAR & RYLANDS, 20, Booth Street, Manchester.
Land Agent: G. W. ORR, Esq., Estate Office, Hilston Park, Monmouth.
'Phone, Skenfrith 4.
Auctioneers' Offices: **6, Mount Street, London, W. 1.**
(Tel. Gerrard 3003-3004).

This sale was only partially successful and a second sale of the remaining 2,323 acres was offered on behalf of Elizabeth Lawley at the Beaufort Arms Hotel in Monmouth on the 4th November. A further sale of 15 unsold lots was held a week later on 11th November.

With Vacant Possession in several instances.

BORDERS OF
Hereford and Monmouth
BETWEEN

THE SALMON RIVERS WYE AND USK

9 miles from Ross-on-Wye, 4 miles from Monmouth (G.W. Rly.), 6½ miles from Pontrilas Station (Hereford to Newport), 16 miles from Hereford.

IN LOTS.   **FREEHOLD.**

The Valuable Sporting and Agricultural Freehold Property

Glenmonnow House

· A GENTLEMAN'S RESIDENCE, occupying a

WONDERFULLY BEAUTIFUL SITUATION

with **126 Acres or 212 Acres,** including **HOME FARM** (in hand) and

Exclusive Trout Fishing in the River Monnow

also

Unsold Portions of the Hilston Park Estate

comprising

16 GRASS AND MIXED FARMS

of from **40 Acres to 368 Acres,** with

Houses and Homesteads, in exceptionally good order
SEVERAL ATTRACTIVE SMALL HOLDINGS

some with Possession on Completion.

and

Numerous Good Cottages, many with Vacant Possession.
Corn Miller's Premises.   Accommodation Lands, etc.,

in and around the Villages of Skenfrith and St. Maughans, the whole extending to about

2,323 Acres.

For Sale by Auction (unless previously Sold Privately), by Messrs.

JOHN D. WOOD & Co.,

At "The Beaufort Arms" Hotel, Monmouth,
On FRIDAY, 4th NOVEMBER, 1921, at 1.30 o'clock.

Solicitor : T. A. MATTHEWS, Esq., 6 and 7, King Street, Hereford.
Land Agent : G. W. ORR, Esq., Estate Office, Hilston Park, Monmouth
(Telephone, Skenfrith 4).
Auctioneers' Offices : 6, Mount Street, London, W. 1
(Telephone, Grosvenor 2130-2131).

Description.				Acres.		
				A.	R.	P.
Lower Dyffryn	...	...	...	368	2	23
Small Holding	...	...	...	2	2	20
The White House Farm	...	...	...	117	0	28
Box Farm	...	...	...	209	2	8
Grazing Farm (Trevonny)	...	...	...	169	3	37
Detached Cottage	...	...	...	0	1	3
Small Holding	...	...	...	38	1	37
Norton Court ...	...	...	...	255	3	0
Ricketts' Farm...	...	...	...	91	2	24
Birch Hill Farm	...	...	...	106	3	11
Detached Cottage	...	...	...	0	2	36
Detached Cottage	...	...	...	0	0	35
Detached Cottage	...	...	...	0	0	26
Pair of Cottages	...	...	...	0	0	32
Meadow Land and Orchard	...	...	...	6	2	4
Cottage, Orchard and Garden		...	...	1	1	1
Dwelling House	...	...	...	0	1	11
Corn Mill and Meadow Land		...	...	10	2	17
Glenmonnow House	...	...	...	125	3	20
New House Farm	...	...	...	86	3	29
New House Wood	...	...	...	10	0	28
Brookland Pasture	...	...	...	14	0	36
Tre-Gout Farm	...	...	...	55	3	25
Barn Farm	...	...	...	102	1	6
Small Holding...	...	...	...	3	1	6
Detached Cottage	...	...	...	0	2	24
Detached Cottage	...	...	...	0	0	33
Upper Linthill...	...	...	...	11	0	15
Lower Linthill...	...	...	...	6	3	3
The Bell Inn ...	...	...	...	6	0	0
Cottage	...	...	...	3	3	30
Small Holding...	...	...	...	7	1	36
Detached Cottage	...	...	...	0	3	30
Carter's Farm ...	...	...	...	77	1	27
Cottage, Garden and Orchard...		...	...	1	2	28
Coxstone Farm	...	...	...	92	0	9
Mixed Woodlands	...	...	...	5	2	24
The Church Farm	...	...	...	185	3	36
Trivor Farm ...	...	...	...	127	1	32
The Old Nunnery	...	...	...	4	1	11
Mixed Woodlands	...	...	...	8	3	36
				2320	0	37

Mrs Lawley sold some of the contents of Hilston house in situ on 12th to 15th April 1921, and included Chippendale and Queen Anne furniture, a Bechstein grand piano, a billiard table and accessories, and three vehicles: a 24hp, six-cylinder charabanc in good running order; a 24hp, six-cylinder, six-seater, La Buire open touring car, recently overhauled, repainted, with a new hood; and a four-ton Foden steam wagon, with a new 13' body, fitted with detached sides, three brakes, a trailer brake and double rubber tyres on the rear.

By Direction of Mrs. E. WRIGHT LAWLEY.

HILSTON PARK, MONMOUTH.

Six miles from Monmouth, 11 from Ross and 16 from Hereford.

Catalogue of the Important Four Days' Sale of the

VALUABLE ANTIQUE AND MODERN

Contents of the Mansion

Including many Examples of Furniture of the period of

William and Mary, Queen Anne, Chippendale, Sheraton, Hepplewhite and Adam Bros.

Numerous finest quality Persian, Anatolian and other Eastern Carpets and Rugs,
Rich Curtains and Draperies,
Boudoir Grand Pianoforte, by Bechstein.
Billiard Table by Burroughes and Watts, with Accessories,
Ornamental China, Fine Bronzes and Clocks,

OIL PAINTING (" The Old Quayside," Newcastle-on-Tyne, by C. Stanfield, R.A.),

Blankets, Bed and Table Linen and Embroideries,

NUMEROUS FINE BED ROOM SUITES & BED ROOM APPOINTMENTS

BRASS AND WOOD BEDSTEADS AND FINE QUALITY BEDDING,

Services of China and Cut Glass,

Sporting Guns, Fishing Rods and Appliances, Ladies' and Gentlemen's Bicycles,

FIVE LA BUIRE & MERCEDES CARS

5-TON FODEN STEAM WAGON, A LATHE and a DRILLING MACHINE

GARRATT 5-TON STEAM TRACTOR

and other Effects, which Messrs.

JOHN. D. WOOD & CO.

Will Sell by Auction ON THE PREMISES,

On TUESDAY, 12th APRIL, 1921,

and Three Following Days, commencing at 12 o'clock precisely each day.

Private View by Order, SATURDAY, 9TH APRIL. :: Public View by Catalogue, MONDAY, 11TH APRIL :: Catalogues 2/- each, from G. W. ORR, Esq., Hilston Estate Office, Monmouth; or from the Auctioneers,

6, MOUNT STREET, LONDON, W.1.

NOTE.—The Fine Sporting Estate of 3,371 Acres, with 6 miles of Excellent Fishing in the River Monnow, and Mansion recently renovated and in perfect order is for Sale. Illustrated Particulars from the Auctioneers.

Ward & Foxlow, Harcourt Street, Marylebone, W.

Records kept at the Royal Commission on Historical Manuscripts, part of the National Archives, show that Elizabeth Lawley was Lady of the Manor of Garway in 1941 and was registered as living at 15 Harewood House, Hanover Square, London. She died in 1968 at the Nyecroft Nursing Home, Bognor Regis.

In her will, dated 10th January 1962, Elizabeth Lawley bequeathed to her daughter, Joyce Wright Lawley the 'three stone diamond ring given to me by my husband on the occasion of her birth' and the sum of £2,000. Elizabeth's furniture, clocks, linen, china, glass, books, pictures, prints, photographs and 'all other articles of personal, domestic or household use', had already been shared between Joyce and her other daughter, Frances Christine Wright Lawley, who also received an income from the estate. Elizabeth also left £4,000, known as 'David's Fund' to be split equally between her grandsons, Peter Delacour de Labillière, Arthur Michael Delacour de Labillière and David Merlin Bennetts.

Sir Peter de la Billière at Hilston Park

One of the Lawley grandsons, General (Retd.) Sir Peter de la Billière, KCB, KBE, DSO, MC and Bar, has visited the house on a number of occasions.

In 1972, at the age of 37, Peter de la Billière took over as Commanding Officer of 22nd SAS. In 1978 he was appointed Director of the SAS and during this time, Peter managed problems in Northern Ireland and dealt with the Iranian Embassy Siege, and the Falklands War. He was Commander, British Forces Middle East, during the Gulf War.

The Bevan family 1921 - 1945

The house, with about 1,000 acres of land, was sold in 1921 to Edmund Henry Bevan, who had been living at Wadhurst Castle in Sussex.

Edmund, the son of Thomas Bevan, a deputy lieutenant of Stone Park in Greenhithe, was heir to a fortune made from manufacturing Portland Cement at Bevan Works in Northfleet, and had at one time been high sheriff for Northamptonshire. He married the Hon. Joan Mary Conyers Norton, third child and eldest daughter of John Richard Brinsley, the fifth Baron Grantley, on 11th February 1903.

They had one son, Bryan Henry, and four daughters, Gwendoline Brinsley, Penelope Joan (later Mrs Vane Tempest), Denise Mary Conyers and Winfreda Irene, (later Mrs Strange), mother of the baby in the photograph taken at Hilston.

Winfreda, the youngest of the family, eloped to Scotland and married a handsome German, named Willy Von-Stranz, changed to Strange at the outbreak of war. Winfreda, her husband and baby were interred for the duration of the war on the Isle-of-Man.

Mrs Joan Bevan was a familiar face as she would often be seen walking around the area, calling on families of the estate for a cup of tea and a chat. She was asked to open fêtes and other local functions and usually walked to attend services at both Skenfrith and St Maughans churches. Before the Second World War, the Bevan family were supporters of the local hunt and point-to-point meetings, taking an active role in rural pursuits. Mr and Mrs Bevan also took part in many parish functions, including Skenfrith Show, which had grown to become one of the best in the area.

Their home, Hilston House, was the venue for a busy programme of social events. On what was then Empire Day, (now Commonwealth Day), pupils from Cross Ash and their headmistress, Olive Martin, would be invited for a picnic on the lawn and a walk around the grounds and garden. Before leaving, they would sing 'Land of Hope and Glory'. An account of Empire Day 1927 was printed in the *Monmouthshire Beacon*. A fête held at Hilston in the early 1920s for the Nursing Association was to fund a motorbike for the district nurse, Nurse Norton. Often events were held to raise money for this cause. Mrs Bevan held regular and popular jumble sales in the large garage at Home Farm. Roley Price of Tre Gout recalled the 'wonderful Christmas parties' at Hilston, to which everyone was invited, and the house also hosted a number of charitable functions. One was a fête held on 9th September 1926 in aid of Llangattock & District Nursing Association. The event was opened by Lady Shelley-Rolls, and featured the Raglan Brass Band, dances on the lawn, and refreshments 'at moderate charges'.

Tragedy befell the Bevan family in 1936, when Denise died after falling from a bolting horse near the Graig House at Cross Ash. She was just 22. According to an account in the *Monmouthshire Beacon*, Denise left Hilston on the afternoon of 15th December to go for a ride on the Graig Hill, accompanied by Miss Doris Biggs of Lettravane Farm, Newcastle. As they were descending the hill, Denise rode on ahead, and her horse gathered speed. Her last words to Miss Biggs were 'I can stop the horse when I like'. On reaching the bottom of the slope, she collided with the wall of the Graig House. A local farm worker, Wilfred James Cornish, witnessed the accident, and went to help. He propped Denise against the wall, then telephoned for a doctor from Monmouth and the district nurse. When Dr W H Williams arrived at the scene, the nurse was already attending to the injured woman, who had a fractured skull and had broken her right arm - evidently in an effort to save herself. She was taken back to Hilston, but never regained consciousness; she died two hours later.

At the inquest the following week, Miss Biggs said that Denise was a poor rider but very keen, and added, 'I noticed that that afternoon she was rather excited'.

The funeral took place at St Bridget's Church, Skenfrith on a Friday afternoon. The organist was Mr Steve Clarke. Officiating clergy were the Very Rev. Dean of Monmouth, Dr J L Phillips, the Rev. Frank Cape, Rector of Welsh Newton, and the Rev. R Oscroft-Jones. The vicar of Skenfrith, Rev. E I Richards, was not able to be present owing to illness. The account in the newspaper records the following employees were bearers at the funeral: Messrs; Alfred Ellis, Ivor Hewlett, Edgar Lawrence and H Vale.

Edmund Bevan died at Hilston on 4th November 1945, aged 83. His estate was valued at £309,730.8s.10d, and was divided between his son Bryan, who had half, and his daughters Gwendolen and Penelope, who got a quarter each. There was also an annuity of £100 for the chauffeur, Ernest Parsloe. Mrs Bevan had predeceased her husband, dying on 22nd July 1942 while receiving treatment for cancer in London. Both Edmund and his wife Joan were buried in Skenfrith churchyard alongside their daughter, Denise.

A member of the Bevan family, Sarah Garlick, from Colinbrook nr Slough in Berkshire visited Hilston in 2004.

Compare this postcard below - showing the ballroom on the left hand side - to the one on page 71 taken before the ballroom and servants' quarters were built.

A postcard sent by Mrs Bevan to Mrs E Pugh wishing seasonal greetings

The Bevan family's last resting place in Skenfrith

Inscriptions on the borders of the grave opposite, see also p 84

Thomas Edward Davies and Meek

After the death of Edmund Bevan in 1945, the Hilston Estate was bought for £36,000 by Thomas Edward Davies, a company director. Mr Davies moved into the mansion with his family in 1946, but his residence was very short – and not entirely beneficial. As soon as he moved in, he sold off all the timber, which included fine old oak and beech trees, for £10,000.

There had been trees lining the road from Crossways to the Old Boot and the drive to South Lodge; travel books published after Davies's time described the area around Hilston as 'utterly devastated'. Later owners of Home Farm, Mr W J B Hall and Vernon Pugh, had the onerous task of removing a large number of enormous tree stumps and restoring the neglected hedges - which had grown upwards and outwards - to their original condition.

Thomas Davies put Hilston on the market on 17th October 1947, the sale taking place at the Beaufort Arms Hotel in Monmouth. Hilston house failed to sell, the bidding started at £40,000 but was withdrawn at £56,000, so the auctioneer offered the house and farms in separate lots. Mr A G Meek of Newport bought the house, South Lodge and Home Farm with 200 acres for £21,500. As well as fishing rights on the Monnow, going for £2,400, he also bought White House Farm for £5,500, Lower Grove Farm for £4,550, and six acres of woodland which sold for £2,395.

The fishing rights, extending down from the weir for two and a half miles, enjoyed some active bidding, starting at £1,000 and finishing at £2,400, purchased by Mr Meek. This lot also included the Freehold of the old Ruthlin Farm House, close to the river which 'could be renovated and converted into a fishing lodge'. The 87-acre Upper Grove Farm at Newcastle was bought by Reg Evans for £3,500 - timber was valued on this property at £1,525 and was to be paid for in addition to the purchase price. The 91 acres that was Tump Farm and included Ruthlin went to £2,700; Woodside Farm's 106 acres was bid to £2,750, but withdrawn; Coed-Anghred farm with 73 acres was sold to G Jones of Bristol for £1825; Cae Graig and 27 acres sold to Mr Ernest Harold Pugh of The Lade for £1,350.

By Direction of T. E. Davies, Esqre.

Monmouthshire

On the Herefordshire Border.

The Hilston Estate

extending to approximately

1088 ACRES

to be offered for Sale by Auction, subject to Conditions of Sale and
unless previously sold by Private Treaty, at

The Beaufort Arms Hotel, Monmouth

On Friday, October 17th, 1947, at 2-30 p.m.

Joint Auctioneers:

Coles, Knapp & Kennedy, Ltd.,
4, St. Mary's Street,
Ross-on-Wye.

Knight, Frank & Rutley,
20, Hanover Square,
London, W.1.

Solicitors:

Messrs. J. R. Jacob & Pugsley,
Abergavenny.

Sale Catalogue of October 17th, 1947

Skenfrith Mill with its eight acres was withdrawn at £1,650, while Mill House, was sold for £900 to Mrs Jordan. Orchard Cottage, adjoining Woodside, was withdrawn at £280. Also withdrawn were Park Cottage at £650 and Laundry Cottage, £350.

Skenfrith Mill

St Fraeds sold to Mr Edgar Edwards for £475; Mr Parry of Crossways bought lot 19, a productive orchard, for £45; the 38 acres of Tower Hill Wood went to Mr Roberts of Mitcheldean for £3,000; Mr Meek bought the 19 acres of Bell Belt Wood and Coed-Anghred Wood for £750, eight acres of Duke's Wood for £270, five acres at St Fraeds Wood for £190 and Kennel Dingle's four acres for £135. Monmouth Steam Sawmills bought Clappers Wood of oak and ash for £2,000; the 17 acres at Colebrook Wood, situated between Lower Grove Farm and the lower road sold for £2,450 to a timber merchant from Craven Arms, Mr Edge. An area of woodland at the north side of Lower Grove, extending to seven acres, sold to a Mr Potter for £850.

Hilston Park near Monmouth © Peter Davies collection

Reproduced by courtesy of Parks and Gardens Data Services Ltd

Particulars.

Lot 1.
(Coloured Red on Plan.)

The Very Attractive Residential Property

known as

Hilston Park

An Imposing Residence in the Classic Italian Style standing on an elevation of 500 feet with commanding views over the Estate.

The House is approached through handsome Entrance Gates off the road leading from the main Ross-on-Wye—Abergavenny Road to Monmouth, by a sweeping drive bordered by a spacious Lawn.

It is substantially built of brick, cement faced with a projecting cornice embellished by square pilasters and a porte-cochere supported by four circular Ionic Columns. An enclosed Vestibule leads through double oak doors to

The Hall

about 27-ft. by 33-ft. with oak block floor and oak panelled walls. Large open Fireplace with Dog Grate. Circular top light.

Cloakroom

leading off the Entrance Hall with tiled walls and rubber tiled floor with Lavatory Basin and separately enclosed W.C.

The Drawing Room

of South Aspect about 32-ft. by 26-ft. 6-ins. with oak parquet floor, elaborately carved plaster panelled walls and a fine moulded ceiling in rope patterns of Fruit and Flowers. Open brick hob grate with marble mantelpiece, with very fine overmantel. French windows opening on to Verandah.

The Boudoir

of South and West Aspect, 20-ft. by 16-ft. with oak parquet floor, panelled Dado, hob grate with marble mantelpiece. French Window leading to Verandah. Very fine overmantel in carved wood.

The Dining Room

of South Aspect, 31-ft. 6ins. by 21-ft. 6-ins., with oak floor, plaster panelled walls and richly moulded ceiling. Open brick hob grate with marble mantelpiece. Flood lighting.

The Music Room

39-ft. x 29-ft. 6ins. with oak floor. Arch ceiling in elaborate panels and partly panelled in oak, and bookcases.

The Study

27-ft. x 16-ft 6-ins. with oak panelled wainscot, and fitted bookcase, oak floor, elaborate plaster ceiling and very fine overmantel in oak.

The Smoke Room

17-ft. x 17-ft., fitted with Mahogany book shelves with Bureau drop desk and very fine ceiling.

5

On the South side is a **Winter Garden** 42-ft. by 20-ft. and a Large **Verandah** about 20-ft. wide with lofty glazed roof supported by fluted columns.

On the **First Floor** approached by a fine Principal Staircase with twisted and turned balusters rising in a central flight to wings on either side and Two Secondary Staircases are:

9 Principal Bedrooms
Four Bathrooms and Three W.C.s

mostly with a South Aspect and with glorious Views, as follows:—

No. 1 DOUBLE BEDROOM (about 23-ft. into wide South bay by 22-ft.) over Drawing Room.

BATHROOM (adjoining) with walls panelled in Marble, rubber-tiled floor, porcelain enamel bath, fitted shower and spray, marble-topped lavatory basin, towel airer, etc., plated fittings.

No. 2 DOUBLE BEDROOM (about 23-ft. into wide South Bay by 30-ft.).

BATHROOM (adjoining) with walls panelled in marble, rubber-tiled floor, porcelain enamel bath, fitted shower and spray, marble-topped lavatory basin, towel airer, etc., plated fittings.

No. 3 BEDROOM (about 20-ft. x 17-ft.) with South and West windows.

No. 4 BEDROOM (about 18-ft. x 12-ft.).

No. 5 BEDROOM (about 18-ft. x 16-ft.).

BATHROOM with tiled walls and rubber-tiled floor, fitted with porcelain enamel bath, Shower, etc., marble-topped lavatory basin with plated fittings.

TWO separate W.C.'s.

No. 6 BEDROOM (about 12-ft. x 13-ft.).

No. 7 BEDROOM (about 18-ft. x 16-ft.).

No. 8 BEDROOM (about 20-ft. x 13-ft.).

No. 9 BEDROOM (about 19-ft. x 15-ft.) with circular bay and window seat.

BATHROOM with tiled walls and rubber-tiled floor, porcelain enamel bath, marble-topped hand basin and heated towel airer, all with plated fittings. Separate W.C.

Practically all the Bedrooms have Central Heating by Radiator.

On this floor there are EIGHT MAID'S BEDROOMS, Housemaid's Pantry, W.C., Bathroom, Heated Linen Room, Etc.

On the Second Floor are TWO BEDROMS.

Domestic Offices

are on the Ground flood level, are light and airy with tiled floors and walls, and include:—

KITCHEN with modern double 'Esse' Cooker.

SCULLERY, MAID'S SITTING ROOM, HOUSEKEEPER'S ROOM, BUTLER'S BEDROOM, STORE ROOM, 3 LARDERS, W.C., GUN ROOM with fitted cupboards.

Outside is a Coal and Wood Shed, Dairy, W.C., Etc.

In the Basement is ample cellage and Boilers for Radiators with a separate automatic Boiler for Hot Water Supply.

6

The Water Supply is an excellent one as stated in the Remarks.

Modern Sanitation Electric Light from new Lister Diesel Plant, 110 volt. 4½ Kilowatt.

Central Heating throughout. Telephone.

The Outbuildings

comprise:—Dairy, 2 Store Rooms, Garage for 5 Etc.

The Grounds

* are laid out in a simple yet dignified manner easy to maintain. There are two Grass Tennis Courts and Spacious Lawns.

A CIRCULAR PAVED ITALIAN GARDEN with Stone Seat.

THE GROUNDS slope down to an Ornamental Lake.

THE WALLED KITCHEN GARDEN approached by an archway with iron Gates is very productive and stocked with the best varieties of Fruit Trees with a fine set of Glass Houses, heated, 2 Peach Houses, Orchid House, 4 Vineries, Forcing House, Heated Pits, Potting Sheds with a well fitted Fruit Room.
There is a Secondary Vegetable Garden adjoining.

At the side of the Entrance Gates in an

ATTRACTIVE BRICK BUILT LODGE

known as

NORTH LODGE

The House is cement Faced and contains:— 2 Living Rooms, Kitchen, Back Kitchen and approached by two Staircases 'are 3 Bedrooms, and Bathroom. Nice Garden.

Electric Light is installed.

This is now held on a Service Tenancy.

Rateable Value of Hilston Park House £180 0. 0.

VACANT POSSESSION OF THIS LOT WILL BE GIVEN ON COMPLETION.

SCHEDULE.

Ord. No.	Description.				Area.
3	Plantation	...	...	...	.697
Pt. 7	Residence and Grounds. Est.		...		10.000
18	Ditto	...	...	...	.282
8	Ditto	...	...	...	.674
17	Ditto	...	...	...	.184
16a	Ditto	...	...	...	.236
16	Ditto	...	...	...	1.699
9a	Ditto	...	...	...	.162
9	Ditto	...	...	...	.549
15	Ditto	...	...	...	.199
10	Ditto	...	...	...	.070
1-4	South Lodge	...	...	...	.290
2	North Lodge	...	...	...	.469
Pt. 878	Pump House	...	...	...	.100
				A.	15.321

A right of way is reserved over Ordnance Number 878 from the Roadway to the Pump House along the track marked with a dotted line on the plan for the purpose of passing and repassing with or without carts, cars or other vehicles. There is reserved from Lots 4 and 11 the right to enter upon these lands to inspect, repair and renew water pipes and Reservoir Tank running thereunder, making good all damage caused thereby.

---

*The details refer to two grass tennis courts, one was in the field overlooking Monmouth

The sale of the Hilston house contents, outdoor effects and cars took place on 11th, 12th and 13th November 1947, after the sale of the house itself. The catalogue provides a fascinating insight into life there in the 1940s.

There were more than 800 lots, which included a Jacobean oak coffer; a 16-inch brass dinner gong on an oak stand; a Steinway grand piano; Turkish and Persian carpets; velvet curtains, lined and interlined; a Georgian gilt gesso bijouterie table - the well top lined red velvet with glazed hinged lid, cabriole legs with female mask terminals, acanthus motifs to feet.

There was a double-barrelled sporting gun; silverware; glasses for brandy, claret and champagne; a 1697 edition of Dryden's Virgil -engraved plates, folio with contemporary calf; more than 30 paintings and watercolours, including Italian School, and Massacre of Children by Roman Soldiers; a sea piece with man o' war firing a salute; dozens of china and ornamental items, including a porcelain octagonal scent bottle and stopper, and a pair of cloisonné octagonal vases with ring handles; a Double Decca portable radio receiver and, intriguingly, an oxygen apparatus on iron stand with castors, and chromium-plated inhaler attached.

Hilston's time as a private residence had come to a close.

By Direction of T. E. Davies, Esq., following the Sale of the Estate

HILSTON PARK

SKENFRITH
NEAR MONMOUTH

Close to main road, between Ross-on-Wye and Abergavenny
10 miles from Ross, 12 miles from Abergavenny, 6 miles from Monmouth

Contents of the Residence

CARS. OUT-DOOR EFFECTS, &c.

which will be Sold by Auction by Messrs.

KNIGHT, FRANK & RUTLEY

in conjunction with

COLES, KNAPP & KENNEDY

on the Premises, on

Tuesday, Wednesday and Thursday

11th, 12th and 13th NOVEMBER, 1947.

At 11.30 a.m. each day

On View: Fri. and Sat. (Nov. 7 and 8), from 10 a.m. to 4 p.m.

Catalogues (price 1/- each) from the Auctioneers:
Messrs. Knight, Frank & Rutley, 20, Hanover Square, London, W.1., or
Messrs. Coles, Knapp & Kennedy, 4, St. Mary's Street, Ross-on-Wye
(also at Monmouth)

Contents catalogue of November 11th, 12th and 13th November, 1947

Part 4

Life around Hilston Park

Tower Hill

A tower that stands above White House Farm, sometimes referred to as a folly, was almost certainly repaired and improved by Cave sometime in the 1840s at the time he created the deer park. But it belongs to an earlier time, perhaps connected to the castle in the valley below. There is no mention of it in the 1838 sale, but it is marked on the Ordnance Survey map of 1843. Recent repairs today have made it structurally sound. It stands about 35' high and measures about 12' in diameter. Originally there was a spiral wooden stairway leading to a top floor from where the estate of Hilston could be seen. The staircase and the brackets on the outside that held the flagpole were still partly in place in the mid-1940s.

This served two purposes; in the early years it was used for observing and probably culling the deer; but it was largely a place where, up to the 1940s (the time of the Bevans), members from Hilston spent afternoons picnicking from the look-out at the top. It is quite possible they refurbished it for this purpose. The Hopkins of Walson, the local builders, can remember updating the windows and the door.

Dorothy 'Dolly' Morgan, now in her 90s, has always lived locally; her grandfather Tom Perkins worked on the Hilston estate for 45 years. She said that the servants would take a picnic up to the tower and the Bevans would walk there.

The late Edgar Edwards of Skenfrith Mill said how he could remember seeing a flag flying from a flagpole secured to the tower, when the family at Hilston were in residence.

The wood that now obscures the building was planted later.

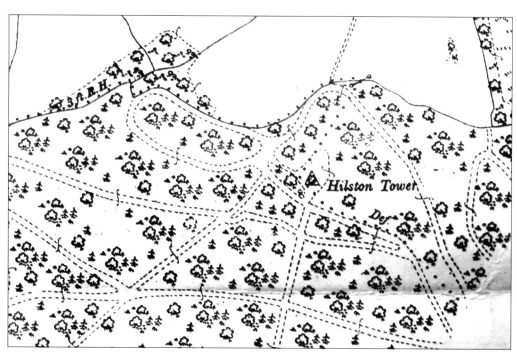

The Barracks

A rare picture of The Barracks, supplied by Rosalind 'Ros' Williams, née Pritchard; a photograph belonging to Danny Williams

The Barracks, or Steward's House as referred to in later sale catalogues, was built sometime after 1821 by Robert Brownrigg, along with two carpenters' workshops and stables with accommodation above. The house was built for the sole purpose of entertaining royalty - who never came. Brownrigg had in his younger days been secretary to The Duke of York, brother of King George IV and had possibly hoped he would be honoured with a visit. The house was pulled down in 1936. It has been thought that this was probably the site of the old house of the Needhams – although this speculation seems unlikely, given the almost universal custom of building a new house on top of the foundations that existed from a previous house, and the fact that a well usually formed part of the foundation. There is also the matter of vistas to remember. It seems much more likely that the Needhams would have been built a house to take advantage of the view currently enjoyed by the present property.

After the devastating fire at Hilston in 1836, the owner at that time, Thomas Coates, lived at The Barracks for a while. In 1960, William Graham, son and grandson of two subsequent owners, wrote:

> In our time, the Rev. Pinney from Llanvetherine came to live at The Barracks for a while with his wife, Caroline, on his retirement. The next occupant of this building was the estate agent Mr Orr. Other staff had quarters at the back.

On the 4th August, 1838, *The Merlin* reported on the forthcoming sale of the estate on 17th August. Divided into four farms of 591 acres within a ring fence, [344 in St Maughans, 247 elsewhere], Mr George Robins was directed to sell by auction at the Beaufort Arms:

> The valuable Freehold property, the Hilston Estate, for many years had stood high in public estimation when it became renowned by Sir Robert Brownrigg bart, fixing on this enchanting spot to retire from the turmoils of public life and dispense.

The Merlin described the stables and Barracks, built by Sir. Robert Brownrigg at the expense of £4,000 as:

> enclosing capital stabling, coachouses, five capital bedrooms for servants, a hay loft, three store rooms, a bailiff's room and two carpenters' workshops.

The Steward's House

stone built and slated, of Georgian character, is conveniently situated near the Mansion House and Stables, and contains on Two Floors: Entrance Hall, Large and Lofty Office, Two Sitting Rooms, Four Good Bed Rooms, Four Secondary Bed Rooms, Bath Room (h. & c.), W.C., Kitchen, Back Kitchen, etc. A separate staircase leads to Two Men's Rooms. Close by are

The Estate Yard Premises

virtually all stone-built with slated roofs, lighted by electricity and in excellent order, having been

RECENTLY THOROUGHLY RENOVATED.

A page from the 1921 sale catalogue

The Stables (1) was next to the site where the Steward's House/Barracks once stood (2).
This building (1) was demolished by Monmouthshire County Council in 1972

Coed Anghred Catholic Church

From a postcard supplied by Bill Price of Skenfrith

The big houses of the area were mostly Catholic and many had their own priest hole, or gave shelter to priests. Hilston was no exception. In 1770, a Catholic priest, the Hon. Francis Dormer, died at Upper Hilston and was buried in the chancel at St Maughans Church.

A picture taken from the same viewpoint with the church picture of page 105 super-imposed; the railings and the base of the large cross matched

Father Abbott, the first priest at Coed Anghred, wrote in a letter in April 1902 explaining why the Catholic church was built:

> There are three places in your immediate neighbourhood where mass continued to be said during those horrible days: The Grove now called New House Farm, [Garway], old Hilston and the Graig; and it was to gather up the remnants of these missions that we opened Coed-Anghred [Catholic Church at Lower Linthill].[1]

This church lies halfway between Hilston and Skenfrith on the old pilgrim road, now called Linthill. Built in 1840 on Coed Anghred Hill, as well as a church complete with castellated tower and bells,[2] there was a house for a priest, a free school and some stables. The foundation stone was laid on 1st August 1844, with *The Merlin* [3] advertising the dedication service for the 22nd September, 1846. However, the Roman Catholic Church was poorly attended; the small school, owing to the lack of pupils, was closed around 1904 with any remaining pupils joining Norton Cross School, one mile west of Skenfrith. As late as 1907, the church only had an income of £80 a year with an average of seven worshippers attending Sunday Mass.[4]

It was decided to close Coed Anghred's Catholic church in 1911 although the cemetery was still in use during the First World War; the church by this time was falling down. The schoolchildren had to walk to Skenfrith Church; although a priest still lived at Coed Anghred. The last marriage there was held on 31st May, 1910; that of Charles William Thomas, of Box Farm, Skenfrith and Margaret Bennett of the Darren Cottage.

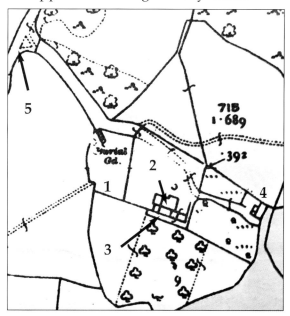

1 Burial Ground. 2 Church. 3 School building and Priest's residence. 4 Stable and barn.
5 Linthill road; note triangular junction for entry from either Crossways or Skenfrith

1. M.N.J (1926) *Bygone Days in the March Wall of Wales*
2. *Monmouthshire Beacon*, 26th September 1846
3. 5/09/1846. The *Merlin* was the forerunner of the *Monmouthshire Beacon*
4. Mary Hopson (1989) *The Roman Catholic burial ground and Former Church at Coed Anghred*

The last burial recorded in the Register Book is that of Patrick Caffrey on 12th July, 1910, but a young girl with the surname Donovan was buried there as late as the 1930s. The cemetery is still there and under the care of Belmont Abbey. On 19th April 1911, Douglas Graham bought the Roman Catholic Church at Coed Anghred from the Monmouth Roman Catholic Charity (1841-1845).

The entrance to the former church premises, now within private ground

The following year, in 1912, at the time he was rebuilding the two lodges, Douglas Graham removed three stone pillars from the church to the North Lodge, and added two more made of brick, and plastered them to match the others, (see page 112). The pillars at the South Lodge, now in private hands, are all brick and plaster. These were modified due to deterioration. The speculation as to whether pillars had been removed from the Catholic Church to Hilston was solved by Roley Price of Tre Gout, who told Vernon Pugh of Home Farm that his father, Ernest Price - colloquially known as Wozzy - had helped remove the pillars from Coed Anghred in 1912 on a long timber wagon that belonged to the estate - Ernest Price was in charge of the buying and selling of animals for the Home Farm. These were

A rare picture showing the demolition in progress around 1921 of the Catholic Church at Coed Anghred. On the right hand side is the school that was attached to the church. From a photograph supplied by Bill Price of Skenfrith

probably the pillars that stood (inside?) the entrance to the church at Coed Anghred. In the 1921 sale of Hilston, brought about by the death of Lawley (see page 74), the Davies family of Cwmyoy bought Lower Linthill, which included the former site of the Catholic Church, (and still does today). They demolished the church and the proceeds from the sale of the stone, windows and doors, paid for the purchase of Lower Linthill. A man by the name of Russell helped to take the church down. Alan Howard, who worked at Hilston and was a son of John Howard the blacksmith at Crossways, helped to remove the stone and brick to Hilston Park and Pembridge Castle at Welsh Newton, with a steam wagon [4] belonging to Hilston.

Some of the gravestones that still exist in the churchyard today

4. Mary Hopson (1989) *The Roman Catholic burial ground and Former Church at Coed Anghred*

Writing in 1974, Jack Axten mentions that a Mrs Preddy, then aged 87, lived near Pembridge at The Pleck where she grew up. She remembered there was a house attached to the Catholic Church built of Bath Stone. On demolition, the marble from the altar was taken to Pembridge Castle for a chapel there and stone went to Hilston. The cross and stained glass went to Monmouth Catholic Church where the glass now forms two windows - previously it was one. Mr Bartlett was the owner of Pembridge at the time. She also remembers two pillars either side of the door, the font was on the right, a stairs to a gallery was on the left and the altar at the far end. There was an organ in the gallery which a Mrs Thomas used to play. Her friend's daughter, Alice James, was baptised there.

Other Catholic churches in the area were at:

-Broad Oak, built in 1846 and closed in 2008. This church may have replaced one at the Grove, now New House, Garway.[5]
-Grosmont, built in 1906-1929. Named St Joseph after Major Joe Radcliff. Built by Count Kyes O'Clery and Godfrey Radcliff (his father). Joseph was killed in the Boer War 1889-90.

Mary Hopson of Tregate has written a comprehensive and detailed account of the church and its records; *The Roman Catholic Burial Ground and Former Church at Coed Anghred, Skenfrith Gwent* and a supplement entitled *Further to Coed Anghred.*

The certificate opposite marks the first Holy Communion of Edith Dorothea Beavan at Coed Anghred Church on Whit Sunday 1900, by Isadore Heneka. Reproduction is courtesy of Mrs Gwen Jones, Cross Ash, granddaughter to Edith Dorothea Preddy, née Beavan. Edith and William Beavan lived at Skenfrith Mill. William had his arm cut off in an accident at the Mill; the arm was buried in the Catholic churchyard. Edith went to school at the Methodist Chapel on the Norton Road.

Thanks also to Frances David

5. WMJ (1926) *Bygone Days in the March Wall of Wales*

The North and South Lodges

The two lodges as we see them today, were completely rebuilt around 1912. The South Lodge, which had been built in the style of a round house with a chimney in the middle, dates back to the time of the Needhams, or earlier. This lodge is now in private hands. The current occupier, Mrs Price, wife of the late Frank Price, is the fifth since the South Lodge was sold off the estate. North Lodge was built later and still belongs to Hilston.

One pillar at North Lodge was knocked several times in the 1970s and 1980s, and cracked. It was taken down to provide a wider access for the school buses and large delivery vehicles in the 1980s. It now lies 15 feet to the east of the present pillars in the undergrowth, see picture below. This was one of the solid pillars taken from the Catholic church, see page 108.

One of the original pillars from the Roman Catholic Church at Coed Anghred, moved to the North Lodge in 1921, now lies in the undergrowth opposite the lodge

Above; South Lodge in 2011. Below; North Lodge in 2011. Inset picture, the North Lodge from an aerial picture taken in 1967 by Skyviews, showing the double pillars either side of the entrance before the one on the left side of the entrance was knocked down

The Rangers, Guides and Brownies

Miss Cora Herring of Blackbrooke, formed a local Ranger Company, with the help of Miss Penelope Bevan of Hilston. The Rangers were firstly based at Blackbrooke, then in Skenfrith Hall. Tragically, Miss Herring died in 1934 at the age of 40 years; a plaque to her memory is in Skenfrith Church.

Miss Cora Herring of Blackbrooke, Captain of Rangers, Guides and Brownies

The Rangers pictured at Hilston Park some time early 1930s. Lavinia Reece is in the back row on the left and May Reece, her sister, is on the right hand side standing

The Skenfrith Ranger Company, photographed in front of an aeroplane on a day out with Miss Cora Herring, their captain

Outside Skenfrith Hall: above (back row l to r) Gwen Pritchard, Frances Hamer, Alice Thomas (her mother was the last organist at the Catholic church) and Prudence Williams. In the centre of those sitting is Laura Wilks with Lavinia Reece on the right.

In the picture below, Lavinia is in the back row right hand side

Pictured in the early 1930s are (back row 4th from right), Elizabeth Irene Morgan of The Firs, later Elizabeth Irene Pugh, The Lade and Lavinia Reece, (seated 2nd from left), Demense Farm   Pictures supplied by Delia Nash, daughter of Lavinia Reece

Dorothy (Dolly) Morgan née Perkins, formerly of The Waen, Cross Ash, was born at the South Lodge. Her grandfather, Tom Perkins, was a worker on the Hilston Estate for 45 years, mostly with the Graham family. Dorothy can remember the Christmas parties at Hilston Park and 'the do's' at the Methodist Chapel at Norton, and Skenfrith Hall. She has fond memories of belonging to the Rangers and Guides. Dorothy recalls how Penelope Bevan carried on after the death of Cora Herring until she married. She had always been affectionately known as 'Miss Pen'. The Rangers continued for a time under the guidance of Lavinia Reece who is the mother of Delia Nash, formerly of Demense Farm, Blackbrooke, Skenfrith.

Other members of the Ranger Company included Denise May and Hilda Wilks

The Skenfrith Girl Guides having a day out.
Lavinia Reece is pictured in the back row 3rd from left

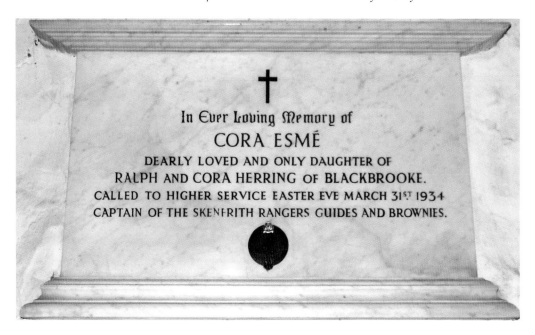

In Ever Loving Memory of
CORA ESMÉ
DEARLY LOVED AND ONLY DAUGHTER OF
RALPH AND CORA HERRING OF BLACKBROOKE.
CALLED TO HIGHER SERVICE EASTER EVE MARCH 31ST 1934
CAPTAIN OF THE SKENFRITH RANGERS GUIDES AND BROWNIES.

The wall memorial in Skenfrith Church to Cora Herring,
located at the back of the church, left of the main entrance

The spot where Cora Esme Herring is buried in St Bridget's churchyard, Skenfrith, Monmouthshire

Second World War Evacuees

A large number of children from Folkestone, Kent, arrived at Troy Station, Monmouth on 2nd June 1940, and after a meal at the Rolls Hall, they were taken to Llangattock-Vibon-Avel School. The placement of children, who were aged between five and 15, was a difficult task, although brothers and sisters were kept together where possible. The largest number were taken to Hilston Park, although this arrangement was not a lasting one - due in part to Mrs Bevan's terminal illness - and children were dispersed to other local families. Mrs Bevan died in 1942 whilst receiving treatment in London.

In the picture: Back row; Miss Hart, ?
Middle row; Margaret Nutley, Joyce Neville, Rosetta 'Rose' Wraight,
Sheila Sewell, ?, two in dark dresses.
Front; Madge Nutley, (extreme left) Phyllis Poppleston, Pat Peel,
Jean Wraight, Pamela Sewell.

Picture reproduced courtesy of Jean Blakesley née Wraight, front row 4th from left

Margaret and Madge Nutley, also Pat Peel, went to Mr and Mrs Davies at Mill Farm, Llanvaenor; Joyce Neville and Phyllis Popplestone went to Mrs Powell, near the Onen; Miss Hart went to Hillside, (Christmas Cottage and now Bryn y Felin, Newcastle); the two Sewell girls were at the Proberts, Pen-y-Lan; Rose and Jean Wraight went to the South Lodge to Mr Bell and his daughters, then Jean went on to Mount Pleasant and Rose on to Mrs Lapworth at Twy Ruddin, the Hendre. Not shown - Mabel and Gladys Nevil who were at Coxston Farm.

Memories of an evacuee: Jean Blakesley née Wraight

My sister and I, along with about 10 other girls, were taken to Hilston Park, owned by Mrs Bevan. The house seemed enormous to us. There were three of us in the bedroom we had, which wasn't too bad.

The first Sunday we trooped off to Skenfrith Church to the service, and did so every Sunday afterwards. We walked down Linthill and back up to our dinner. We walked everywhere then. There was no school bus and we went to Llangattock School which was very crowded with all the newcomers. On the way home, we stopped at a bank where wild strawberries grew and picked some handfuls. The lake also came in for a visit as we were from the seaside [Folkestone] and loved water.

We were lucky at Hilston in that there was electricity and hot water from their own generator. Most houses had only well water for drinking and water from a rainwater butt for washing. Water was carried in galvanised or enamel buckets and kept in the pantry for cleanliness. On one occasion I was taken by one of the maids to the Home Farm where, for the first time in my life, I saw hens and ducks, all running free, and I fed them corn.

We ate our meals in the servants' big room and I can remember that we all had our sugar ration in little jars. One day, one of the maids looked out of the window and said there was a soldier coming down the drive. We looked and, without asking if we could leave the table, my sister said, 'come on Jean, it's our dad' and we were gone. He had come to make sure we were being properly treated.

We were moved out of the big house to more homely houses in the area; my sister and I went to Mr Bell the gardener and his two daughters, Annie and Edie at South Lodge, (see page 131).

Life at Hilston

The Flower Show

In 1876, Hilston hosted a flower show that subsequently became an annual event, and grew in size to the extent that it was transferred to the Weir Holme Meadow in Skenfrith. In the sale of Hilston Park in 1921, the 14 acre Brookland Pasture (Weir Home Meadows), was sold for £500 to Alton Court Brewery, with the agreement that the owner of Hilston can hold Skenfrith Show on six consecutive days during any week in August.

The foxhounds

In 1913, Douglas Graham started a private pack of foxhounds known as The Douglas Grahams. Dick Partridge of Bacton, with the approach of war, asked Douglas if he would take charge of his pack of hounds; this he did. The hounds arrived at Hilston in 1913 and were housed in a compound at Dreinos Wood near Highland Cottage (formerly the Poplars), Crossways and a large enclosure was built at Kennel Cottage (now Park Cottage), Crossways. A year later, Douglas too joined the army and passed the hunt

Park Cottage, Crossways, previously known as Kennel Cottage and Lower Laundry

Highland Cottage, formerly The Poplars on the Linthill road from Crossways

to Captain Nugent Hope, of Whitney Court who rehoused them at Bacton and changed their name to the Golden Valley Hunt. Captain Dick Partridge was killed in September of 1918,[1] Douglas Graham returned to Hilston. The Hunt is still in existence, now based in Brilley, Herefordshire.[2]

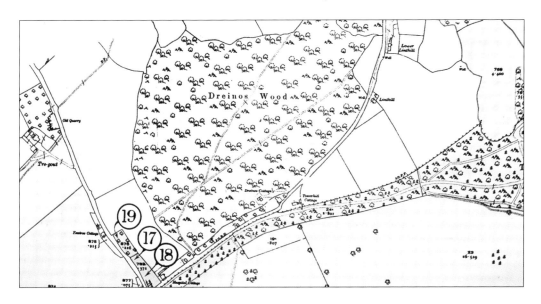

1. He was awarded the Military Cross for 'conspicuous gallantry and devotion to duty' and the French Croix de Guerre was also awarded. The latter being notified in the London Gazette for 8th October, just after his death near Havrincourt Wood on 28th September, 1918. Captain Partridge is buried at Beaumetz Cross Roads Cemetery, France and is also commemorated at St. Mary's Church, Abbeydore, close to Bacton

2. These extracts are from the book by William Bailey, *Partridge Hounds; The Bacton Hunt* (2004), courtesy of Tony Lane of Eardisley.

Living off the land

All the houses and cottages on the estate had large vegetable gardens with chickens; some had a pigsty. Many farmers supplemented their income by selling rabbits and in many parts of the country, rabbits were farmed in warrens, although Hilston does not appear to have had one. In hard weather, Hilston staff would feed swedes to the estate's many rabbits, which formed a basic diet for the estate workers and others. A wood on the estate below Lower Grove, called Clappers Wood, derives its name from the Old English clapper, which means rabbit burrow.

The Hilston Greys

The estate had four Percherons for work horses, known as the Hilston Greys. Their names were Bonnie, Bright, Flower and Surly. The Percheron is a breed of draft horse that originated in the Perche valley in northern France. Percherons are usually grey or black in colour. Originally bred for use as a war horse, they are well-muscled, and known for their intelligence and willingness to work. There were several grooms and over 16 horses [2] used for hunting at Home Farm. Theopolis Smith, pictured below, was a horse doctor living at Broad Oak, who travelled around the area on horseback, visiting places around Skenfrith, Cross Ash, and large houses including the Waen. In many instances, owners would collect Mr Smith from his home when extra equipment was needed. It is very likely he was called upon to look at the numerous horses on the Hilston Estate.

2. These hunters would have been commandeered for the First World War, many of the hounds would have been put down

The Staff

Between 1908 and 1919

Mr Betteridge, the head coachman, lived at Park Cottage, once called Lower Laundry Cottage and Kennel Cottage. Mrs Neighbour, a widow, was the laundress and lived in Deri; Tom Perkins in Laun, (Laundry Cottages). Alfred Thomas Perkins (known as Tom) was, for 45 years, a waggoner at Hilston and won many prizes in the Llangattock-Vibon-Avel and District Agricultural Society ploughing and hedging matches that were often held at Home Farm. Tom lived for some years at No 1 Smithy Cottages before moving to the South Lodge. He had three children, Harry, Annie (born 1903), and Jim; his parents lived at Crossways Cottage. He died aged 93 at Comas Cottage, (off the Norton to Grosmont road towards Cross Ash). Annie Perkins, his daughter, continued to live there up to the 1970s.

This picture is of Tom Perkins, a waggoner on the estate for 45 years. Inset, Annie Perkins, his daughter

Frank Jones the gamekeeper, lived with his family - Jim, Jack and Ivy - at Gamekeeper's Cottage also know as Dreinos Cottage, The Poplars and (present day) Highland Cottage. Living opposite, at Tower Cottage, was the electrician, Mr Isacs, (sic) with his wife, two daughters and a son.

Mr Ellis, the gardener, lived at Lilac Cottage, Mr Winter lived at Holly Tree Cottage and had two daughters.

Mr Long the carpenter, lived at Caldy House, he had two boys and two girls. Mr Howard was the blacksmith and lived at No 2 Smithy Cottage, with his 17 children. Mr

Holly Tree Cottage (left), and Lilac Cottage, Crossways

Thayer the cowman, lived at No 1 and had four daughters. Mrs Richardson lived at Upper Linthill with her daughter. Mr Kedward lived at Lower Linthill and had a horse and trap hire business; it was two shillings to Monmouth and two shillings back. George Gale junior was bailiff to James Graham, and lived at Trevonney Farm. The bailiff at Hilston between 1913 and 1919 was a Mr Orr, who lived at the Estate House (The Barracks). Mr Birkett was the head gardener and lived at the Stables, next to The Barracks.

© Peter Davis Collection
parksandgardens.ac.uk

Two gardeners pictured against the south wall of the garden at Hilston Park

THE GLASS HOUSES

(all heated from two stoke holes with modern boilers) comprise: Two Newly Erected Peach Houses, Orchid House, Four-division Vinery, Plant House, Fernery and Three-division Forcing House. There is a Range of Heated Pits, Fruit Room, Potting Sheds, Store Rooms, etc.

© Peter Davis Collection
parksandgardens.ac.uk

One of the gardeners with the melons grown in one of the many greenhouses
Top; an extract from the 1921 sale catalogue

Thomas Lawrence, right, head gardener at Hilston, grandfather to Irene Lawrence, a housemaid and father to Edgar Lawrence, below, electrician on the estate and former blacksmith.

The Head Gardener's House

is stone built and slated, and contains Three Bed Rooms, Sitting Room, Kitchen and Scullery. Adjoining is the BOTHY, comprising Kitchen and Two Bed Rooms.

Between 1920 and 1945

After the First World War, economic activity was at a low ebb; many of the horses used in agricultural production had been taken off the farms for use in the First World War, the ones that were left were getting old. Many of the men had been killed, estates had to manage the best they could. Hilston Estate was the largest employer in the St Maughans and Skenfrith area as food production on the farms was critical to the revival of rural fortunes. Mr Bevan employed a chauffeur, Ernest Parsloe, who worked for him for 45 years until the time of his (Parsloe's) death. Parsloe lived in the 'new houses' built by Grahams in Crossways, next door to Edgar Lawrence. Other employees of the time included electrician Edgar Lawrence, (pictured above left) bailiff Lloyd Price, butler Charles W Tuck, gamekeeper Robert Cornwall, mason William T Hamer and the cook Dora Barnes. Robert Cornwall, in the late 1930s, used to have broody hens from Mrs (Elizabeth) Irene Pugh of The Lade - who kept about 1,000 laying hens - to hatch out his pheasant eggs.

Edgar Lawrence with his wife Lucy, eight year old daughter Irene and baby son Walford sitting on the wall at the Blacksmith Cottage in Crossways circa 1928. Irene and Walford both went to Norton School. Walford then went to Monmouth School and on leaving, served an apprenticeship in the West Midlands where he became a planning engineer

Picture courtesy of Irene Williams née Lawrence, the little girl on the left

Crossways Cottage, formerly Gipsy Cottage, much enlarged since the days of Alf Ellis. The original cottage started on the right of the picture and ended at the chimney.

Alfred Ellis, brother to Reg (?) Ellis of Lilac Cottage, Crossways, died in January 1947, aged 73. He had worked on the estate for around 50 years, and was known for his skills as a woodman and forester. Alf, as he was known, lived at Crossways Cottage, with his wife, two daughters and one son. His wife played the organ for Sunday School at the Wesleyan Chapel, later The Methodist Chapel and now a house called Brook Cottage.

The Pheasantry

The Pheasantry was situated near to South Lodge; Mr Arthur Matthews lived there. His son, George Matthews was later to become well known as a resident of the Laurels Cottage near Cross Ash and was a regular winner at flower and vegetable shows in Cross Ash and Monmouth. The house is now called South Villa, formerly Park Villa and was also the home of the Lawrence family who worked on the estate. Present owners are Carol and André Lines who have been there for the last 41 years. The pheasant pens were still there when they moved in, and they believe that hounds were kept in a smaller building to the side.

The Pheasantry, looking south. These photographs are supplied courtesy of Carol and André Lines

South Lodge, circa 1920
picture courtesy of
Irene Williams

Mr Bell, who lived at the South Lodge with his two daughters, are pictured below
with Rosetta 'Rose' Wraight, see page 120.

Mr. Bell the gardener

Annie and Ede Bell with
Rosetta centre

1 and 2 Smithy Cottages and blacksmith shop (foreground), at Crossways, Monmouthshire

The carpenter at Hilston was George Hopkins who later, along with his sons Clifford, Jack and Wilfred, started a business at Walson, branching out to become the local undertaker. Clifford Hopkins retired to Monmouth.

One man with a long connection to Hilston was Ernie Parry. He came to work at Hilston after leaving school, and lived in the bothy at Home Farm with two other boys. His father, Harry Parry, was the local stonemason and lived at Coed Angred. One of Ernie's daily tasks was to take milk to Glanmonnow; he also became a postman and part-time gardener. During the Second World War, he worked at the munitions factory in Hereford. Later, he worked for the War Agriculture Executive Committee (colloquially known as the War Ag), then came back to Hilston to work as head gardener until his retirement. He bought Caldy House (the old hospital) and lived there until his death. Ernie began work at the estate when Arthur Lawley was there. 'He never turned anyone away who was looking for a job,' he said many years later. 'Even though there was not much to do, Mr Lawley would give us a billhook each and tell us to go and cut some thistles in the fields. He would often come down and have a chat to us while we worked; he was a very nice man.'

Memories of Hilston; Phyllis Gordon (née Jones)

Phyllis Gordon lived at the Top Shop, next to the churchyard in Skenfrith, and can remember her time at Hilston Park between 1937 and 1940; during the time of the Bevan family.

Phyllis Jones, pictured in front of the lake at Hilston in 1938
Picture courtesy June Morgan

I went to Hilston in 1937 and at that time, there was just a great open range in the kitchen. On that, all the cooking was done for the three family [members] and ten staff. All the wood and coal was carried out manually up from the yard by the little hall boy - the scullery next to it was a dark damp miserable place for a fourteen year old girl to work in.

They did not stay long. The bedroom that I shared with my friend [Irene Lawrence] was looking towards Crossways with the big tree outside the high window - it is still there. The servants' hall was opposite the back stairs. One big scrubbed table and ten hard chairs. That was all the furniture - not even a mat on the floor, just a sink in the corner. The kitchen staff ate in the kitchen mostly and the butler, lady's maid and cook would eat in the housekeeper's room which was opposite the butler's pantry - the footman washed the delicate china and the silver. These staff spent most of the time polishing the silver. The footman's bedroom was next to the large walk-in safe. His room had a window opening out onto the conservatory (not changed). He was supposed to guard the safe. The young boys I saw there would have run a mile if challenged.

The house is little changed. The rooms and the floors were beautiful, thanks to our efforts - coal fire in the study, wood fire in the drawing room, none elsewhere. The lady of the house was the Hon. Mrs Joan Bevan, née Norton, daughter of the notorious Lord Grantley [John Richard Brinsley, 5th Lord Grantley, Baron of Markenfield]. Her husband, I think, was a gentleman formerly. Mr Bevan saw to the running of the estate. Mr and Mrs Bevan both had a tool like a walking stick with a v-shaped appliance on the end - she called it her 'spudder'. With these, they would spend hours on the estate digging up thistles. They had produced four daughters and a son. The third teenage daughter, Denise was killed while learning to ride a horse. Winfreda, the youngest, eloped to Scotland and married a handsome German, Willy Von-Strang. On the outbreak of war, the name was changed to Strange and she and her baby followed him to the Isle of Man where they were to stay for the whole of the war. The parents [Bevans] died during the war and lie within a gravestone in Skenfrith, next door to my home [Top Shop, Skenfrith]. My ancestors lie near-by - no class distinction in churchyards.

I don't think that war made much difference to them. They were almost self-supporting except for petrol. The bailiff and his wife made butter and cheese in the dairy at the Home Farm. Plenty of milk, beef, lamb and poultry around; and firewood. The butler lived in the North Lodge with his wife. He spent nearly all his time at the big house. On his half day off, he used to go back up for his meals. The head gardener lived in the South Lodge with his two spinster daughters. There was a smithy at Crossways, it is now an extension to Smithy Cottages. Also a laundry, that is now two cottages called Lawn and Derri, [now Laun and Deri].

Laun and Deri Collages ut (Lower) Crossways, formerly Laundry Cottages, front and (inset) back

The blacksmith became the electrician [Edgar Lawrence]. My uncles tenanted two of the estate farms, The Tump and Woodside - my uncle was able to buy Woodside. A well kept drive ran through the canopy of Beech trees up to the South Lodge - ruined by a subsequent owner who just bought the place for the timber I heard.

The Mill and the Mill House belonged to the estate and almost most of Crossways. I was glad I didn't live in an estate house - if they saw the tenants talking together, they would be reprimanded for gossiping. There was a chapel - never used - near the oak room, the big room near the conservatory. The field between Hilston and Crossways was called the Hospital Meadow. In 1940, I left and got a job on the buses, much more fun.

Phyllis Gordon, known then as Phyllis Jones, was a maid at Hilston in the years between 1937/38 and is pictured third from left, with other members of staff. They are on the steps in front of the conservatory at Hilston. Irene Lawrence is second from left (see also page 137) and married Cecil Williams, the footman, the man in the centre of the picture. John Goodman, became footman after Cecil Williams.
Picture supplied by Jean Ridley, daughter to Phyllis Gordon

Memories of Irene Williams née Lawrence 1926-1941

Irene Williams, now in her 90th year, can remember living at the Pheasantry. 'I was only a little girl when we lived there (also known as South Villa and Park Villa). We moved afterwards to the 'new houses' at Crossways. My dad, Edgar Lawrence, was the local blacksmith. When I was six years old, I went to Norton School, and dad used to take me to grandad's [Thomas] house, [No 2 Smithy Cottages] where I waited to go to school; dad then would open up the blacksmith shop. Grandad had a housekeeper who made huge loaves of bread and she used to cut me a slice, butter it and sprinkle it with sugar! With fewer horses to shoe, dad became the electrician on the estate. He had the job of working the big machines at the [farm] buildings; the steam engine [puffing billy] used in the sawpit;

pumping the water from the pumphouse, and starting the generators that charged the batteries in the big house. When I married Cecil, he was in the army so I lived with mum and dad, next door to Mr Parsloe the chauffeur. His wife was a dressmaker - spending a lot of time in London - and used to make dresses for the Bevan girls.'

Irene 'Rene' Lawrence and Cecil Williams on their wedding day at the 'new houses' in Crossways in 1941 and, inset, celebrating their 60th wedding anniversary. Irene, now a widow, lives in Crosskeys

Irene Lawrence in front of the rose garden at Hilston. The stand for the statue behind her was found in a ditch in undergrowth on the Home Farm some years later by Vernon Pugh and is pictured right

In the 1921 sale of Hilston Park, the estate yard premises are described as having;

Boiler and Engine Houses with 10 h.p. Marshal boiler and a $6^{1/2}$ h.p. steam engine which drives a Parker dynamo, generating the electric light and also shafting for sawing, lathe, etc.; two Battery Houses of 56 cells each and resistance board for charging car batteries, Cider House with mill and press, Weigh-bridge, Blacksmith's Shop, Saw Bench Shed with rail runway, Covered Sawpit, Carpenters' and Painters' Shops, Timber Drying Shed, etc.

Monmouth Archaeologist Steve Clarke said that his grandfather, Frank Clarke, was a gardener at Hilston Park Estate sometime in the 1940s. By this time, they were living at Cae Graig, as Frank had formerly been a gardener at Blackbrooke Estate; his wife had been a cook there. Steve said that all the local lads who were off to war held a party in Skenfrith and it was agreed that they would all meet again when the war was over. 'They all came back to the return party except one - my father's twin brother Harold who died with all hands on HMS Manistee, fighting U-Boats in the North Sea - they've spelt his name wrong on the Skenfrith War Memorial. Dad joined Bomber Command and took part in the thousand bomber raids - but got home safely.' Frank may well have worked alongside his dad on the estate as it was he who recalled the gardeners/servants bowing out of respect as the owners passed.

The Lake

The report of the fire of Hilston House in 1836, page 54, refers to:

> [A] line was formed for the purpose of conveying water in buckets from the pond on the premises but on account of its distance there was not so abundant supply as could be wished

proving there was some form of water enclosure at that time. When George Cave bought the estate in 1838, he effectively rebuilt the house and grounds as we see them today. It is also quite possible that, to ensure a good supply of water was on hand in case of another fire, he enlarged and defined the boundaries of the lake with a stone revetted wall, which can be seen when the water levels are low. He may have, at that time, drained the lake and lined the bottom with clay. Vernon Pugh can remember a clay pit in the Pumphouse field (opposite the North Lodge) that was about 20 yards square and about four feet deep.

Apart from the two islands and the grotto that can be seen today, there was also a boathouse with a stained glass window that was still there in the 1950s, but only the foundations remain today.

The lake has been dredged twice in living memory. Once partially in 1962 when a dragline excavator was used to clear the sediment, and again in the late 1990s when a diaphragm pump from Robert Price of Abergavenny pumped out the lake and an excavator dragged the sediment onto the side of the lake.

The picture above shows the boathouse in the 1920s, and below, a picture taken in the 1980s. When the boathouse was intact, a small pipe, now gone, over a stone sink had a small flow of spring water flowing continuously (spot marked X below, left side, centre)

An opening at the lake's water line, referred to as a grotto in the Cadw report, page 166, takes the curious only about 10 feet in, and is often flooded when the water level is high

The Monkey Puzzle trees at the lake's edge and, right, an entrance at the northwest edge of the lake off the drive to the South Lodge with a young Henry Pugh

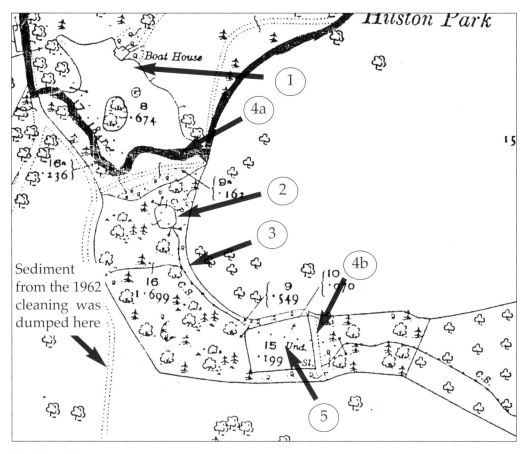

Sediment
from the 1962
cleaning was
dumped here

1 - Boat House
2 - holding pond
3 - overflow stream
4a and 4b - sluice gates
5 - lily pond

There were originally two
sluice gates, one small one
at the lake's water edge (4a)
- now gone - and the other
much larger one, 4b, is still
in the wood below the lake.
When the lake was drained
(for cleaning) the lower
sluice gate was opened at
the same time so that the
draining lake water would
not overcome the lily pond.

Part 5

A new era begins

Hilston School 1948 - 1991

A report in March 1948 proposed a school for children with special needs at Hilston Park. The Sites and Building subcommittee of what was then Monmouth Education Authority decided to buy Hilston House with 15 acres of surrounding land for a special needs school. Mr Edwards was appointed to run the school, engage staff and supervise the layout. The *Monmouthshire Beacon*, reported on the scheme in a March 1948 edition when Mr Edwards became headmaster for a short while. The school underwent some alterations, making it safe and secure. Ernie Parry, the gardener for many years, spoke of a tunnel in the underground passages being sealed up for safety reasons.[1] Fire escapes were added at both ends of the building. The outside and inside toilets were updated and the kitchen was modernised. The lake was fenced off, although later removed; part of it still remains on the park side, now the farm land.

Eric Earl arrived as headmaster from Beacons School, Lichfield, on 29th December 1956. For the first few years, there were three other teachers, and a roll of around 45 boys. Eric Earl was assisted by his wife Frances, who was appointed matron and was responsible for the pupils' welfare outside school hours. She had male and female care staff to help her. Dr Eric Old, a Monmouth doctor visited every Thursday morning for a routine check on the boys' health.

Douglas 'Doug' Davies was appointed deputy head, and his wife Joan was made assistant matron. Colin Lewis, Bill Bailey and other members of staff were appointed. Doug and Joan lived in a flat at Hilston, and stayed until the school was relocated to Chepstow in 1970. They and their three sons then moved to Scotland, where Douglas was appointed head of a school for boys at Killearin, near Glasgow. Bill Bailey moved to Peterchurch, Dorstone, and took up a teaching post there. Two members of staff, Heather Williams, (now Mrs Warren Davies) and Josephine Morgan (now Mrs Gordon Higginbotham) were resident in the staff quarters during term time. The staff rooms were next to the Davies' flat.

1 Could this have been the last remnants of a time when persecuted Catholics had a form of escape in penal times

Hilston Park School staff and boys in 1962

Josephine Morgan (Higginbotham)

Walter Higginbotham

Mary Watt

George Edmunds

Ernie Parry

May MacIntyre née Little

Joyce Hughes née Cleaves

Masie Simmonds née Bradley

Elsie Evans

Bill Bailey

Colin Lewis

Doug Davies

Still living in Monmouth, Joyce Hughes can remember her time spent working at Hilston Park and the friends she made there.

'Walter Higginbotham the driver, used to come in to Monmouth and pick me up outside Sterrets, (now Ruby Tuesday) along with my friend Evelyn Crouden and take us out to Hilston to work, then drive us home to Monmouth. May MacIntyre's maiden name was Little, her parents had Little's butcher shop in Monmouth. Beryl Ruck did the laundry, Elsie Evans was the cook and George Edmunds worked in the garden alongside Ernie Parry. It was a nice crowd to work with, the boys there were lovely. My duties were general housekeeping; making beds and cleaning. I used to pick flowers from the garden to put in the vases.'

Her daughter, Valerie (now Lewis), remembers going to the Christmas parties held there, with her sister Marion when they were eight or nine years old. Valerie's husband, Ray Lewis, who played for Monmouth School football team, can remember going out to Hilston Park to play matches against the Hilston boys; 'the boys from Hilston always won!', he said.

'There was a rumour that Cliff Richard was going to buy the mansion at one time, but he never did' Joyce added.

Mr Dan Williams came to Hilston in January 1959 as teacher of general subjects and to develop the pupils' interest in music. He extended the pupils' vocal and instrumental skills through contact with local church and chapel, which helped the school integrate with the local community. After a time, Mr Williams also gave lessons in woodwork, and he and a group of woodwork pupils made a scale model of Skenfrith Church. He later became senior teacher, he retired in 1977. Colin Perrott joined the school staff in 1962, his main duties were involving the outdoor activities.

Hilston Park 1962 to 1970.

1962; Memories from teacher Colin Perrott

I took up my teaching post at Hilston Park Residential School in September 1962. I lived in for the first term there while I looked for accommodation for my family. Whilst the room was comfortable it was fairly basic and designed to accommodate the 'sleeping in' member of staff. This provided the overnight supervision mainly regarding fire regulations. Because of this duty, I got to know the layout of the building extremely well. The bathroom I found very substantial, with all the paraphernalia that suited the distant past residents - it was a bit flamboyant for my needs! The first classroom I was allocated was on the ground floor, at the southern end of the building and was roomy and light and suitable for our needs - mine and the pupils.

Amongst my responsibilities were the gardening lessons and I spent a considerable amount of time outdoors. I enjoyed the locality with its sweeping views and interesting panorama. The gardening lessons took the form of projects. We extended the size of our main growing plot and also constructed a goldfish pond complete with a waterfall activated by a submersible pump. We also added flower beds to various suitable sectors of the surrounds. The formal walled garden was worked by the Local Authority gardeners. The produce was sent to various authority establishments, including the school kitchen. The gardening group had access to some of the facilities on the site and some plants were obtained from the garden.

Indoors, especially at Christmas, a great effort was made to give the children a happy and exciting time. I was in charge of decorating the entrance hall and main staircase, as well as the main passageways. The structure and furnishings of these areas enhanced our efforts and stimulated our minds. Staff also co-operated in constructing a model church which was placed on the front lawn. The building was completed with stained glass windows depicting nativity scenes. Appropriate music was also broadcast from the church. On a clear, frosty night, the atmosphere created was inspiring. In all, the house, its structure and position had many advantages for a residential establishment but the drawbacks were becoming evident and sometime after I left, the school closed and was replaced in Chepstow by a modern building more suitable to the changing needs of the type of education that was being established.

Hilston Park 1970 to 1991

In 1970, when Hilston Park ceased to be a special school, teachers and pupils were transferred to Castle Hill School, a new, purpose-built establishment just outside Chepstow. The Earls stayed with the pupils as head and matron until their retirement.

Hilston was empty for roughly a year, but in September 1971, the house and grounds re-opened as an Outdoor Education Centre (OEC) for secondary school children in what was then the county of Monmouthshire. In 1973, with the redrawing of county boundaries, Monmouthshire and Newport were merged to form the county of Gwent. Mike Oxford was appointed as head of field studies and biological science. Bryn Tucker joined in 1972 and took responsibility for outdoor activities.

1971; Memories from teacher Mike Oxford

In 1971, I was appointed to Monmouthshire County Council as adviser for biological science and field studies, from my position as senior lecturer at the City of Birmingham College of Education, having previously taught at grammar schools in Hampshire and Kent. At this time, Hilston Park was to be set up as a field study and outdoor pursuit centre, to cater for secondary school groups on a weekly basis. My responsibility was to oversee the centre and the academic programme of work, covering areas of biology, geography and geology, history, and environmental study. I was also to be resident at the centre, which added a family aspect to the appointment.

Outdoor pursuit programmes were supervised by county physical education staff. Domestic staff who had previously worked at the special needs school returned, as they lived in the local area or Monmouth. These included Lorna Davies from Newcastle, Mrs Frank Edmunds of Crossways, Phil Blakesley of The Lade (part of Home Farm), and John Barnes from Llantilio Croesenny.

Staff between 1973-88 included; left to right, Mary Barnes, Lorna Davies, Mrs Frank Edmunds and Maisie Thomas

From the beginning, my emphasis was on work in the local area, as the centre was ideally suited for this. Close working relationships were built up with farmers, landowners and local individuals, such as Bill McAdam, vicar of Skenfrith and Grosmont. A large range of week-long programmes was devised, including hedgerow, woodland and freshwater studies from a biological point of view, and land use and farming studies – using Hilston Park's Home Farm with Vernon Pugh, White House Farm with Jimmy McConnel, and Llanrothal Court's Frank and David Breakwell. All of these people were exceedingly co-operative, and generous with their time and information. Drainage and fieldwork studies also involved Norton Court and Nant-y-Ych, as well as Hen Gwrt at Llantilio.

Village and town studies too played a very important part in study programmes, with a local trail being devised as an introduction to the area. Skenfrith, Grosmont, Monmouth and Abergavenny were all used as study areas for settlement – in particular the latter for market surveys in agricultural studies. Being within the area of the Three Castles – Skenfrith, Grosmont and White Castle – historical settlement was also well covered. My role as adviser for biology and field studies also demanded work in all schools in Gwent; I was able to organise courses for teachers, using all of the great diversity of countryside and individuals mentioned above – and not least stops for lunchtime refreshment at the Bell, the Wellington and the Angel!

John Barnes began work at Hilston Park in 1969; his duties were driving the school utilabrake, stoking the central heating system, attending to water and sewage systems, general maintenance of buildings and routine attention to the school vehicle. He spent the first 18 months working under Eric Earl. When the school transferred to Chepstow in 1971, he and eight other staff were taken each day down to Castle Hill School to train the Chepstow staff. After nine months, he finished at Chepstow and returned to Hilston in the September. His post was re-designated in 1979 and his duties then included gardener, handyman and driver and his hourly rate was then fixed at £1.3351 per hour. John's wife, Mary also worked there, in the years between 1973-88 and his aunty was Dora Barnes, a cook in the 1930s (page 128). John finally retired in 1993.

John Barnes manning the tuck shop in the 1980s

1972; Memories from administrator Bryn Tucker

I was appointed to Hilston Park Centre from 1972 up until September 1991. At that time, the Centre had been operating as a weekly residential centre for secondary school pupils from the county of Monmouthshire. My appointment enabled students to have a wider choice of activities, which could include outdoor pursuits in the form of hill walking, rock climbing, canoeing and caving, in addition to Field Studies.

Staff at Hilston in the 1980s included (l to r) Brian Cavill, Chris Blumer, Nigel Reed and John Barnes and (not pictured) cook Joanna Jones and secretary Kathy Bowen

During the nineteen years I spent at Hilston Park, a whole variety of activities were catered for, from five-day and weekend courses for primary and secondary school pupils to holiday and weekend visits from groups affiliated to the Royal National Institute of Blind (RNIB); Physically Handicapped and Able Bodied (PHAB); Women's Royal Voluntary Service (WRVS); painting groups and even, on one occasion, a lace-making group, where the tutor was embroidering the fleur-de-lis that would form the cushion cover on which the wedding ring of Prince Charles and Lady Diana rested. An addition to the facilities offered at the centre was a caravan club park location within the walled garden – the highlight being the annual visit of the Sunseekers Club.

For the first year, groups of around 48 children, accompanied by their teachers, could visit the centre from Monday to Friday, when the students would undertake a field study, an environmental study or an outdoor pursuits course designed by the school staff. On the retirement of Mike Oxford, Bryn Tucker became head of Hilston and Forest Outdoor Education Centres (OECs) until his retirement in 1991, at which point it was passed to Alan Wilkinson, who became responsible for the four outdoor centres run by Gwent County Council, which now included the Trefil and Talybont OECs.

1991 to present day

Left to right; Ian Kennett, Richard Gledhill, Jan Evans,
Sharon Rainford and Alan Pocock

Ian Kennett

Ian Kennett, has been Head of Service since 2004. Prior to that, he taught at Hilston from 1991, and before that, was at Trefil Mountain Centre between 1989 and 1991. He has overall responsibility for the Hilston Park Outdoor Education Centre (OEC), Gilwern OEC and Talybont OEC. Around 30 staff are employed between the three centres, and the service has an annual turnover in the region of £850,000.

Every year, around 1,500 people visit and stay at the centre at Hilston. Most are school groups, but some are youth and adult groups. Since Hilston became an outdoor education centre, around 60,000 people have made use of the facility.

Monmouthshire Beacon

www.monmouth-today.co.uk

Established October 1837

FOREST OF DEAN GAZETTE — Wednesday 26th January 2011 Price 40p

Another victim of cuts?

Hilston Park Centre, one of the buildings that could see budget cuts hitting pupils

by Desmond Pugh
despugh@tindlenews.co.uk

A PRESTIGIOUS outdoor education centre may have to close its doors if its funding is cut.

If proposals by Newport City Council go ahead, a knock-on effect could cause Hilston Park to put up its prices or shut altogether. The Gwent Outdoor Education service, a collaborative arrangement between Blaenau-Gwent, Newport, Monmouthshire and Torfaen, has been in place since 1996 and has enabled all four partners to provide a high quality, cost efficient, locally-based service at a relatively modest cost. This service is now under threat after Newport City Council's cabinet proposed cuts to their education budget. Current support from primary and secondary schools within Newport is strong, with 43 out of 49 primary and secondary schools being regular users. Annually, the outdoor service provides over 19,000 user days, of which over 6,000 are provided to young people from Newport.

Head of Services Ian Kennet told the Beacon: "Should Newport withdraw financial support there could be a number of potential knock-on effects.

Continued on page two

The main current issue is funding. As local authority funding of the outdoor service is reduced (frozen since 2005 and reduced more severely since 2008), keeping the service going is increasingly difficult. Hilston is a large building to oversee; repairs are always needed; heating and insulation are not very efficient, therefore fuel use is high; its listed status makes any work more expensive than that on a normal building; and the building's very size makes even an ordinary job more difficult and expensive.

If financial cuts bite deeper, we may well need to close one of the centres, (Page One, *Monmouthshire Beacon*, 26th January 2011). Hilston is really the jewel in the crown, so is relatively safe, but the service is not just one centre.

Hilston continues to be very popular with all groups, and we get a never-ending supply of people (often delivery drivers) who reminisce about their time here. The atmosphere and setting are unique, and the centre is about as good as it gets for a residential outdoor education centre. I've not seen anything that betters it in the UK.

Ian Kennett

Former Heads of Service

Prior to Ian, head of service from 1999 to 2004 was Dean Ryan. Before him, Alan Wilkinson was head, starting with Gwent around 1970. Alan was in charge of Trefil and Talybont OECs at the same time that Bryn Tucker was in charge of Hilston and Forest OECs.

When Bryn retired, Alan took over as head of all four sites, and saw the service through the most difficult period in its history: local government reorganisation of 1996. In that year, Gwent was devolved into five unitary authorities: Blaenau Gwent, Caerphilly, Newport, Monmouthshire and Torfaen.

Alan managed to get four of the authorities (Caerphilly withdrew from the service) to agree to create a joint service to enable the outdoor centres to carry on in much the same way as they had prior to reorganisation. The legacy he left was a very cost-effective and efficient service, with a strong client base and good links to local schools and youth organisations. Many of the systems he designed and set up are still in use.

Present day staff

Jan Evans, Administration Officer - in post since 1993, is a key member of the service. The entire service relies on Jan very heavily. She oversees administration of every booking at all three centres – in the region of 220 per year – and deals with around 250 school and youth organisations, processes all invoices, all payments and all staffing returns so people get paid at the end of the week.

Richard Gledhill is the site coordinator. Based at Hilston since 2004, he has been with the outdoor education service since 1991. He is responsible for the day-to-day running of the centre, arranging details of all visits and teaching of groups.

Also employed at Hilston are outdoor tutors Rick Walker and Dan Thorne; domestic staff Mary Ruck (whose mother also worked at Hilston for many years), Julie Knight, Sharon Rainford and June Morgan (whose mother, Dorothy was in service at Hilston circa 1925); and maintenance officer Alan Pocock.

Features of the building

Some of the decoration designs on some of the ceilings at Hilston are thought to be by Eric Gill and his brother, MacDonald.[1] The Oak Room, or Ballroom as it was formerly known, pictured below, is part of the servants' quarters that were added around 1912, during the time of the Gills. MacDonald Gill's ledger entries relating to Hilston Park show no visit to Hilston, just drawing work done for Hilston in November 1911 (total of 53 hours work is noted). Eric's diaries (in the Tate Library on microfilm) mention work at Ditchling on a fireplace for Hilston. The figures refer to hours spent on job. Entries read:

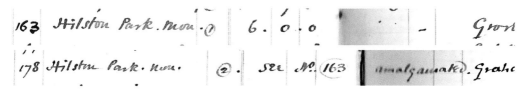

April 21 Sun Grove (Hilston) in morn 4 hours (at Ditchling)
April 22 Mon Grove re Fireplace (Hilston) 6 hours
April 24 Wed Grove Hilston Fireplace 3 hours

1.Detective work by Caroline Walker, with thanks to Richard Gledhill
The ledger entries and diaries belong to Andrew Johnston who inherited them from Max's second wife when she died. Reproduced courtesy of Andrew Johnston

Pictures of the Oak Room, with designs thought to be by the Gill brothers

Caroline Walker is MacDonald (Max) and Eric Gill's great-niece. Her grandfather Evan Gill was one of their younger brothers. She has been researching the life and work of Max Gill for the last five years and is currently writing a biography. She was co-curator of a major exhibition of Max's work at Brighton University in Summer 2011.

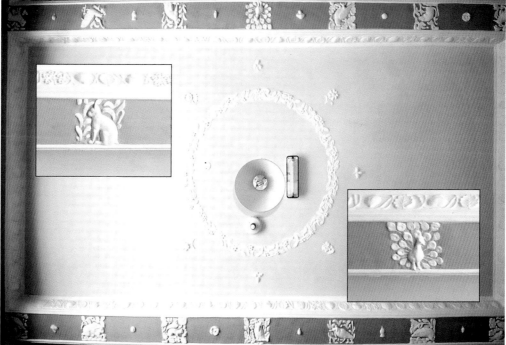

Other decorative ceilings are found throughout the house. Here the picture, top, shows the games room, formerly the drawing room and, lower, a bedroom ceiling, quite likely a child's room at one time with insets showing some of the figures

The former nursery bedroom has an ornate cast iron fireplace of the type being made by the Blaenavon Iron Works at the time when the house was built and has the following rhyme engraved on it:

The fire my glittering father is,
Th'earth my mother kind,
The sea my younger brother is,
But me no man can find.

An Italian marble walled bathroom has a large bath surrounded by a maze of pipes supplying water to a Victorian shower. All the water for the house was heated by a large wood burning boiler which needed constant attention

Some interesting wall paintings were revealed when wallpaper was stripped off the Boudoir wall. These paintings of a country gentleman, two cherubs and two hunting birds are at ceiling level. Experts from the National Library at Aberystwyth have visited the house but have not been able to advance any firm opinion about them.

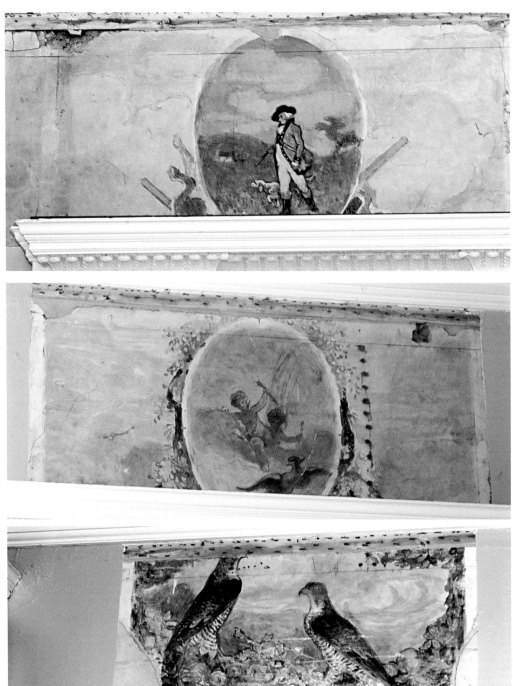

APPENDIX

i: Bibliography

ii: Floor plan of Hilston House present day

iii: CADW / ICOMIS report

iv: An architectural summary

v: Register records for Catholic Church

vii: Registers for St Maughans Church

vii: Landholdings for Duchy of Cornwall-1610

i

Bibliography

Bailey, William: *Partridge Hounds; Otherwise Known as the Bacton Hunt 1907 - 1914, Herefordshire.* Berrington Press, 2004

Bradney, Sir Joseph: *The Hundred of Skenfrith.* 1904

Burke, John: *Genealogical and Heraldic History of the Commoners of Great Britain and Ireland.* 1826

Catholic Record Society: *Recusant Rolls,* v. two. 1989

Charles Coxe: *An historical tour in Monmouthshire.* 1801, volume two.

Hopson, Mary: *The Roman Catholic Burial Ground and Former Church at Coed Anghred, Skenfrith Gwent.* 1989

Hopson, Mary: *Further to Coed Anghred.*1994

Hopson, Mary: *A Wander Round Llanrothal.* 1987

James F. Jamison: *The Descendants of John and Catherine Marr of Kittery.* 1985

Kissack, Keith: *Monmouthshire Houses*

Levett, Fred: *The Story of Skenfrith, Grosmont and St Maughans.* 1984

M.N.J.:*Bygone Days in the March Wall of Wales.* 1926

Newman, John: *The Buildings of Wales: Gwent/Monmouthshire.* pp524-525

Paul, Sir James Balfour: *Scots Peerage.* 1904 Founded on Wood's Edition of Sir Robert Douglas's Peerage of Scotland, v. five and nine

Williams, John: *Llyfr Baglan 1600-1607.* 1910

Survey of the Duchy of Lancaster 1609-13

ii

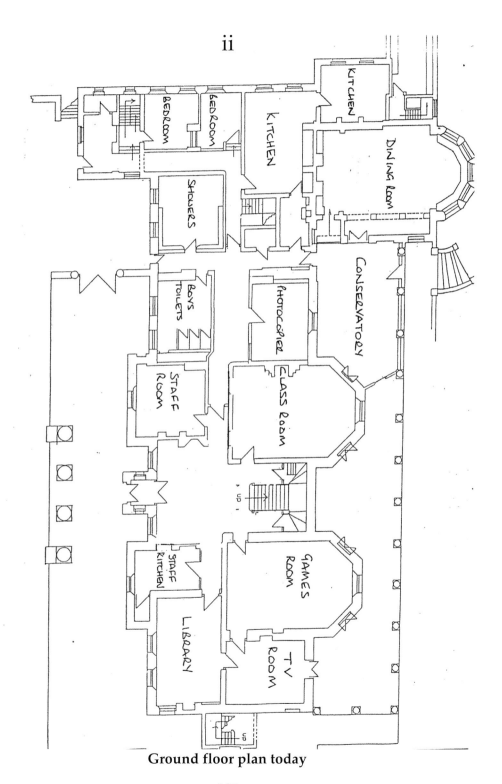

Ground floor plan today

iii

CADW/ICOMIS Register of Parks and Gardens of Special Historic Interest in Wales

NAME: Hilston Park
REF. NO:. PGW (Gt) 22OS
MAP: 161 GRID REF. SO 446187
FORMER COUNTY: Gwent
UNITARY AUTHORITY: Monmouth B.C.
COMMUNITY COUNCIL: Llangattock-Vibon-Avel
DESIGNATIONS: Listed building: Hilston House Grade II National Park
AONB SSSI NNR ESA GAM SAM CASITE EVALUATION Grade II
Primary reasons for grading 19th-century park and garden, with some well preserved features, including ornamental lake and folly tower.
TYPE OF SITE: 19th-century landscape park, pleasure grounds and garden; 19th-century walled kitchen garden, ice-house
MAIN PHASES OF CONSTRUCTION:c. 1840 onwards
VISITED BY/DATE: Elisabeth Whittle/December 1990
HOUSE Name Hilston House Grid ref SO 446187
Date/style: c. 1840/neo-classical

Brief description: Hilston House stands on the top of a ridge to the west of the Monnow valley. There has been a house on the site since at least the 17th century. During the 17th and 18th centuries it was owned by the Needham family. In 1838 the house was burnt down and the next owner, Mr. Cave built the present one, which is a large neo-classical, two-storey building. The main front is on the NW, where there is a two-storey portico in the centre. The SE front has a single-storey portico running the length of the front, leading to a conservatory at the NE end. The E wing of the house was added in the early 1900s.

OUTBUILDINGS
Name: Coach-house
Grid ref: SO 445188
Date/style, and brief description: The coach-house stands on the NE side of the drive, between the drive and the Home Farm. All that remains of it are the back and side walls. The rest was pulled down in 1972.

THE PARK

Central grid ref: SO 450l85

Date/style: Mid l9th century/landscape

General description: History, and layout

The park was made at the same time as the house was rebuilt, c.l840, by Mr. Cave. At the beginning of the 20th century his plantations were 'now just coming to their prime' (Bradney). It is a small, modest landscape park on rolling ground sloping to the south,to the west of the Monnow valley. Its chief ornamental features are the plantations, and it is now largely in agricultural use. The house stands on the highest part of the park and from it and the garden most of the park can be seen (facilitated by a ha-ha on the edge of the garden).The house stands in the western half of the park, with entrance drives to the NW and (a longer one) to the S of it.

At both entrances, there are gates, gate piers, and a two-storey classical lodge. The tarmac north drive winds through a wooded area to a level forecourt of grass with a rectangular tarmac area in front of the main entrance to the house. The south drive skirts the forecourt to the N and sweeps round southward past the lake and straight to the B4347. This drive is now reduced to a farm track.

The park is largely in agricultural use (mixed pasture and cultivation), with plantations mainly along the watercourses in the western part. (The lake at the head of the watercourse on the W side of the park is within the garden/pleasure grounds.) Below the lake, in a belt of woodland, is an artificial pond, now more or less silted up. In the north-east corner of the park the ground rises to a small hill overlooking the Monnow valley. On the top of this hill, in the middle of a wood (mostly former Forestry Commission plantation, planted in about 1960), is a circular stone folly tower (Hilston Tower), which may be slightly earlier than the park, possibly dating to the end of the 18th century. It is three storeys high, with an open top, and windows and an entrance on the ground floor. Holes for floor joists and stair treads are visible, and a down-pipe is exposed in the wall, suggesting that there was originally a roof.

STRUCTURAL COMPONENTS

Drives:

N drive: a short tarmac drive on the NW side of the house. Winding past woodland and the Home Farm to the E and an area of woodland to the W, and arriving at main front of house, where rectangular tarmac area surrounded by lawn.

S drive: a longer drive to S of house. Gravel, used as farm track. Curves around N side of forecourt to join N drive in front of house. W side edged with ha-ha (low revetment wall and ditch) N of lake, where drive forms the boundary between park and garden. In the north-east corner of the park a track leads off the small lane east of Crossways (SO 451193) eastwards through woodland to the top of the hill, where there is a folly tower (Hilston Tower). The track passes this, and runs in a loop to the west of it. This was presumably a carriage track to the tower. It is now very overgrown in places, and is virtually impassable.

WATER FEATURES

Several springs in the park (mainly in the western half) give rise to watercourses which run eastwards towards the R. Monnow. That in the NW corner of the park flows directly into the lake. Below the lake, in woodland, is a small artificial pond, now more or less silted up.

BUILT FEATURES

Lodges:

N lodge: Two-storey neo-classical building on the W side of the N entrance (private house) S lodge: (SO 444181) a two-storey neo-classical building on the W side of the S entrance (private house), similar in style and size to the N lodge. Gates and railings

N gates: Rendered square gate piers with small ball finials. Side pedestrian gates on both sides. Iron gates, and iron railings both sides. On W side of S drive (N of lake) iron railings and iron posts with chains between them, set into revetment wall (some posts fallen).

S gates: Similar to N gates.

Hilston Tower(SO 458194)

This is a three-storey folly tower built on the top of the hill in the north-east corner of the park. It is probably of late 18th century date. It is a tall circular tower built of roughly coursed old red sandstone, with patches of rendering on the surface. The tower appears to have been built with two different red sandstones - the stone on the northern side has weathered much more badly than that on the south. The base is slightly wider, with a dressed stone top. The top is open, and there are no internal floors, although holes for floor joists and stair treads are visible. The entrance is on the N side, and is a wide opening with a horizontal lintel. Four wide windows are spaced at regular intervals around the ground floor. Horizontal wooden lintels survive on some. Higher up the walls there are narrow slit windows. Although no roof survives there is evidence that there once was one in the form of a down-pipe in the thickness of the wall, now exposed in one place.

PLANTED COMPONENTS

The trees on either side of the N drive are mainly deciduous (oak, sweet chestnut), with an underplanting of evergreen shrubs.The plantations are of mixed deciduous and coniferous trees.The wood in the north-east corner of the park is now largely modern coniferous plantation (Tsuga heterophylla, planted in about 1960; about to be felled).

BOUNDARIES

W side: drive and field boundary N side: road, track, field boundary E side: field boundary S side: track, field boundaries

ESSENTIAL SETTING, VIEWPOINTS AND CONTINUATIONS OF FEATURES BEYOND THE PARK, EYECATCHERS ETC.

Essential setting: farmland to E, S and W of park View: S from SE front of house and garden (A on map)

LAND-USE Agricultural: pasture and cultivation Woodland: unmanaged

ELEMENTS OF BOTANICAL OR OTHER NATURE CONSERVATION INTEREST

None known

SURVIVAL OF INDIVIDUAL COMPONENTS

Structural components: all

Water features: most

Built features: all

Planted components: most

THE PLEASURE GARDEN

Grid ref SO 446187

Date/style c. 1840 and later/formal; pleasure grounds

GENERAL DESCRIPTION AND LAYOUT

The garden and pleasure grounds lie to the SE and SW of the house.They were made at the same time as the house was rebuilt in c. 1840 by Mr. Cave. The garden lies to the SE of the house, around which is a flagstone path. Below this is a levelled lawn bounded by a grass scarp. Two grass paths at the W end of the lawn lead down the grass slope W of the house to the lake below. To the E of the main lawn is a further lawn (formerly tarmac), to the NE of which is the overgrown Italian rose garden, a roughly circular area surrounded by a low clipped yew hedge. Remnants of formal planting, such as single cypresses in the angles of the W and S sides, are visible, but the interior is overrun by seedling trees. In the middle are the remains of a circular stone-lined pool and fountain. To the south of this area, in the corner of the garden, is an area of tangled yew and deciduous trees, beneath which is a subterranean icehouse. Only the top of its entrance on the E side is visible. The garden is bounded on the E by a stone revetment wall, and on the S by a ha-ha opposite the house and an iron fence on the slope to the west. From the S front of the house there is a panoramic view of the park. There are a few ornaments in the gardens, including two cast iron urns on cast iron square plinths (the urn and plinth of one have become separated). To the SW of the house is a larger and more informal part of the gardens - the pleasure grounds. Below the house is a grass slope with a few specimen trees in its northern half. Two grass walks lead down this slope to a wooded area in a small valley, in which is an artificial lake, dammed at its southern end. The stone revetted lake has a very sinuous outline, with a long inlet on the W side, at the end of which are steps up to a rustic stone arch leading to the S drive. There are two stone-revetted islands, the larger kidney-shaped, the smaller circular, both of which are ornamentally planted with evergreen trees and shrubs. On the E shore of the lake is a ruined stone boathouse, approached by stone steps, and a simple domed alcove 'grotto' set into a rustic stone wall. The woodland around the lake is planted with a mixture of deciduous and coniferous trees and shrubs, including pines, cypresses, monkey puzzles, copper beech, yews and laurels.

STRUCTURAL COMPONENTS

Terraces and paths:

A wide grass terrace on the SE and SW sides of the house, c. lm. below house level. Above it on the SE side a flagstone path runs the length of the portico, outside it. There is a 0.6m. high scarp at the outer edge of the terrace. On the SW side of the house the flagstone path has a 3-sided central projection with a corresponding step below it. At the E end of the SE front of the house steps and a flagstone path lead round the SE part of the house. There are two grass paths leading to the pleasure grounds: one at the NW end of the terrace on the SW side and one on the SE. The first runs straight from the W corner of the house down to the boathouse on the lake. Just above the boathouse the path is sunken and curved. The second is a curving grass path below the terrace on the SE side which runs down to the S end of the lake through a shrubbery.

Ha-ha:

The ha-ha forms the boundary between the SE garden and the park. Its drystone wall is about l metre high, and is in fairly good condition. At its E end it continues as a low stone wall, which is ruinous along the NE side of the garden. On the W it ends at the end of the terraced lawn, and an iron fence continues the boundary between pleasure grounds and park down to the lake.

Water features:

At the foot of the grass slope to the SW of the house is the lake. This is artificial, fed by a spring at its N end, and dammed at its S end by a massive earthen dam across the valley floor (one known leak). Its maximum dimensions are c. 100m. N-S and 60m. E-W. In shape it is very sinuous, with curving inlets all around, and a long narrow inlet on the W side at the end of which are steps to a path leading to a rustic arch to the S drive. The sides are revetted with sloping stonewalls (ruinous in places), and there is a stone sluice and overflow channel on the S side. In the centre of the lake is a kidney-shaped island, also with a sloping stone revetment wall round it. Between it and the E shore is a smaller circular island, similarly revetted, with the faint trace of a path running E-W across it between two rows of golden cypresses. There are signs that these islands were linked to each other and to the shore (circular island-E shore) by bridges, now gone. On the E side are a boathouse and grotto (see Built Components).

BUILT COMPONENTS

Steps:

Concrete steps down to terraced lawn on SE side at E end of portico. Stone steps down same slope at E end of flagstone path.

Lake:

3 stone steps in sunk path down to boathouse. Flight of 14 stone steps on W side, at end of inlet.

Walls:

On the W side of the lake, reached from the lake by steps, is a rustic doorway leading to the S drive. It is built of large irregular stones, with a large stone lintel across the top. The NW side of the Italian rose garden, SE of the house, is bounded by a low drystone wall.

Boathouse:

On the E side of the lake, N of the islands, is a ruined boathouse projecting into the lake. It is built of stone and is reached by a narrow sunken path. The slope above the boathouse is revetted with a wall c. 2.2 m. high. In front of this is a U-shaped 'harbour' with a narrow ledge around it of dressed stone. On the N side there is a rectangular stone projection into the lake with a bath-sized sunken pit in it. The roof has disappeared.

Grotto:

Between the circular island and the boathouse the lake is revetted with a vertical wall of large irregular stones c. 2m. high. In the middle of this wall is a semi-circular alcove with a lintel of rougher stones. It is c. 1.8m. in height, 2.5m. in depth and 1.2m. in width across the entrance. The interior surface is of the same stone as the wall.

Icehouse:

In the SE corner of the garden, in a very neglected and overgrown area of trees (evergreen and deciduous) and shrubs, some fallen. It is subterranean, with its top showing as a low circular mound above ground, very overgrown, with a large leaning yew tree on top. The top of the entrance is visible on the E side, the rest blocked up with earth and debris.

ARCHITECTURAL ORNAMENTS

Paving:

A stone flagged terrace around the SW and SE sides of the house. Stoneflagged path below steps at E end of terrace, running around E end of house.

Plant containers:

Two cast iron (painted white) urns, with intertwined handles and heads in relief on the sides. One stands at the W end of the forecourt on a rectangular iron plinth (also painted), underneath it is a well. The other stands, without its plinth, in the middle of a millstone just to the S of the ruined coach house. Its plinth stands in the SE corner of the garden, near the icehouse.

Stone plinths:

At the N end of the terrace to the SW of the house are three low stone plinths, c. 0.6m. high, two on either side of the top of the grasspath, and one further N. On their tops are the stubs of missing stone ornaments. On the W side of the entrance to the Italian rose garden is a circular stone plinth, c. 0.7m. high, with an iron tenon in its top.

Bird bath:

Below the centre of the terrace SW of the house is a circular stone bird bath, c. 0.8m. in diameter.

Pool and fountain:

In the centre of the Italian rose garden to the SE of the house are the remains of a circular stone pool and fountain. Both are very overgrown, and only the rolled lip of the pool is visible. Parts of the fountain remain but are not visible.

PLANTED COMPONENTS

Pleasure grounds:

The pleasure grounds lie to the SW of the house. The eastern half is a large grass slope with a few specimen trees in its N half, in particular a Wellingtonia and a Lime, both large, mature trees. Along the southern boundary is an area of shrubs and trees, mainly rhododendrons, with the trees including a large cedar. The western half of the pleasure grounds is taken up with the lake and its surrounding woodland. The woodland planting is ornamental, with a mixture of deciduous and coniferous trees and an underplanting of evergreens such as laurel. Near the SE corner of the lake is a large mature beech; along the S side are Pines and Cypresses, on the W side are two large Monkey Puzzle trees, and N of the steps on the W side is a large Copper Beech. The large, kidney-shaped island is planted with Cypresses, Yews, and Portugal laurels (some recently cut down), and the small circular island has five Golden Cypresses in two rows either side of the path that crosses the island. The sixth has been cut down, and its stump remains. Evergreens(Yews, Laurels etc.) are planted above the boathouse.

Garden:

The garden lies on the SE side of the house. Most is taken up with a large terraced lawn, with a further lawn (formerly tarmac) to the E, on the edge of which is a large Sweet Chestnut tree. In the SE corner of the garden is a neglected area of evergreen (Yew) and deciduous trees, some of which are fallen. The door into the kitchen garden, E of the house, is flanked by a large Yew on the E and laurel on the W. On the NE side of the garden is the Italian rose garden, a roughly circular area surrounded by a low clipped yew hedge. The whole area is overgrown and neglected. The entrance is by a flight of shallow steps in the NW corner, to the W of which is a Yew tree. The hedge has angled protrusions in the middle of the W and S sides, in the angle of which are single Cypress trees. There is a further Yew tree at the end of the hedge on the E side. The interior is overrun by seedling trees.

Reconstructions of original planted features: None.

Special collections of garden plants: None.

Documented living plants: None.

Other (including elements of nature conservation interest):

The grass slope to the W of the house, in the Pleasure Grounds, is a plant conservation area, maintained to encourage wild flowers (cut once a year).

ESSENTIAL SETTING AND VIEWS BEYOND THE SITE

Essential setting: park to E, S and W view out S from terrace of house and S lawn of garden across park (A on map).

ANY SPECIAL FEATURES; None

SURVIVAL OF INDIVIDUAL COMPONENTS

Structural components: most.

Built components: some

Water features: most

Architectural ornaments: some.

Planted components: most trees, some shrubs.

UTILITARIAN GARDENS

NAME Kitchen garden

Grid ref SO 447188

Date/style 19th-century/walled kitchen garden

DESCRIPTION (categories as for the pleasure garden)
The large walled kitchen garden stands to the NE of the house, E of the entrance forecourt. It is rectangular, and is orientated SW-NE. The walls are of red brick, mostly c. 3m. high (c. 2m. to the E of the door on the S side, E wall c. 2.2m.) with a flat capping. They are in good condition. The N wall and the N end of the E wall are whitewashed and the N wall is buttressed. There are entrances on the W (two, one door and one wider gate with plain square gate piers and double wooden doors), N (door), E (door near N end) and S (door into the garden). The door into the garden is arched, with a wrought-iron gate in it. The interior (used in the summer as a caravan park) is grassed over, with a few isolated old fruit trees remaining, some of which are in rows, indicating the line of former paths.
The ground slopes gently towards the S. In the S corner an outbuilding extends slightly into the garden. A cross revetment wall divides the garden in two, c. two thirds of the way towards the E end. It is a low stone wall, c. 0.8m.high, with a flat stone capping and two flights of steps down to the lower eastern part of the garden. The steps have been rebuilt recently. There is a NW-SE scarp c. l.5m. high across the middle of this part. To the N of the kitchen garden is a narrow area between the N wall and farm buildings in which there are ruined lean-to sheds and glass-houses. This area is very overgrown, with dismantled glasshouses, lights etc. piled up all over it.
SOURCES
Primary:
Catalogue of contents of the mansion for sale, by direction of Mrs E.Wright Lawley, l92l: Newport Reference Library (pqM 447.5 645)
Secondary:
J. Bradney, A History of Monmouthshire, Part I, p. 57.

Reproduced by kind permission of CADW

iv

An Architectural Summary

The Buildings of Wales: Gwent/Monmouthshire,
John Newman
pp 524-525

A major early Victorian stuccoed classical mansion, about which little is known. It was built soon after 1838 for a Bristol banker, George Cave, and completed for John Hamilton (a tall, needle-like polished granite obelisk commemorating him stands in the churchyard of St Meugan). The two-storeyed N front is dominated by the mighty pedimented porte cochère of four giant Greek Ionic columns. The front is of nine bays, the outer pairs slightly recessed, which further emphasises the portico. Coupled antae demarcate angles. Uniform entablature all across. The S front, by contrast, has two full-height polygonal bays flanking a narrow centre with niches. Later full-width, single-storeyed colonnade, its entablature and fluted Ionic columns entirely of cast iron. Large early C20 additions towards the E. They consist of a N-facing service block, two-storeyed and pedimented on paired pilaster strips, and a S-facing single-storey ballroom with round-headed windows in its polygonal S end. A decorated rainwater head here is dated 1912. The architect of the ballroom at least seems to have been Arthur Grove.

To the S, semicircular lawn as wide as the house. From it a magnificent panoramic view of the Monnow Valley opens out.

Internally, the plan of the ground storey, completely symmetrical, is probably of the 1830s, but the house was redecorated throughout for James Graham in the first years of the C20. The front door leads into a hall, heated from a heavy stone chimneypiece to the L, with big consoles. Wainscot reported by Bradney to have been brought in from Lower Dyffryn, Grosmont, in 1902.

Beyond, the toplit staircase rises on axis. It is on the imperial plan, rising in one flight and returning in two. Two balusters per tread, one turned, the other twisted. Large round-headed openings above on all four sides, some glazed, some blind. The square top light over the stair, linked by spandrels to a glazed oculus, looks like a survivor from the 1830s house, similar to that over the stair at the Shire Hall, Monmouth, by Edward Haycock.

The main downstairs rooms are all decorated in a handsome early C18 Baroque style, with marble chimneypieces, large-fielded panelling and enriched plaster ceilings. The ballroom of 1912, for Mr Graham's son,

Douglas William Graham, is quite different in style and much more idiosyncratic. In fact it is a full-blown display of Arts and Crafts decoration and spatial manipulation. Plasterwork takes pride of place, broad bands of oak leaves traversing the broad span of the coved ceiling. Signs of the Zodiac follow the line of the cove on the tympanum which closes the ceiling at the S end. W arcade of three semicircular arches on square, wainscoted piers, forming an aisle or vestibule towards the adjoining conservatory within the E end of the cast-iron colonnade. At the N end, an elaborate inglenook centred on a chimneypiece with polished fossily stone slabs radiating above a hearth flanked by cheeks of brown mottled tiles.

Upstairs, a nursery, clearly by the same designer. Plaster ceiling decorated with animals, fruit and leaves. The fireplace here is lined with metal cheeks embossed with a poem about the four elements. Shallow bow window and a seat all around it. Nothing else upstairs deserves a mention except another early C20 feature, twin marble-lined bathrooms, one each side of the staircase well.

Two early C20 stuccoed lodges, one at the N end of the front drive, the other 1/2m S, on the B4347, clearly by the architect of the service wing of the house. They are a pair and unusually elaborate, two-storeyed on a Greek cross plan. Full-height paired pilaster strips frame sash windows. Complicated hipped roofs.

V
Registers for Coed Anghred Church

The Register book of baptisms, confirmations, marriages and deaths of the former church at Coed Anghred is kept at St Mary's Catholic Church, Monmouth.

The baptisms start in 1846 (five recorded) and finish in 1908 with the baptism of Lawrence Cuthbert Phillips. Confirmations begin in 1871 (seven recorded). Edith Dorothes Beavan's confirmation certificate (page 111) states she was baptised at Coed Angred in 1900, although Mary Hopson records she was confirmed at St Mary's in Monmouth.

Marriages began in 1852 and finish in 1910.

Some of the more interesting headstones at Coed Anghred included:

-Charles Porter who died May 16th 1881 aged 69yrs. Also Sarah his wife (of Skenfrith) who died May 22nd 1889 aged 64 yrs. Also Thomas their son who died June 8th 1860 aged 8 yrs

-George Henry infant s/o Henry Charles & Mary Jane Weetman died May 29th 1884 aged 6 days

-In mem of William son of Joseph & Jane Roberts of Llangattock Vibon Avel who died July 22nd 1856 aged 84 yrs

-In loving memory of Patrick Garrett only son of Peter & Margaret Caffrey [of 29 Monnow Street] who died March 1 1896 in his 12th year

Side 2. Jeremy Peter Patrick Caffrey who died July 9 1910 aged 69 (Mr Caffrey was newsagent in Monnow St, Monmouth in 1885)

-Jane Mooney who died at Coed Anghred June 9th 1870 aged 68 yrs

-In loving memory of Edwin Prosser late of Lower Lint Hill died 30 Nov 1896 aged 66. Erected by his son Tom.

-Ann Catherine wife of Charles Bastock, died March 16 1909 aged 69. Also their son Francis Joseph born June 8th 1881 died February 22nd 1891. Bastocks lived at 25 St James Square Monmouth

-John Charles Segrave late of H.M. 4th Regt of Foot. eldest son of O'Neil & Frances Segrave who died at Croft-y-Bwla Monmouth December 29 1853 aged 24

Side 2. O'Neil Segrave, Captain H.M. 13 Light Infantry. brother of the above who died at Croft-y-Bwla August 8 1860 aged 27, (Croft-y-Bwla is a farm on the Rockfield road out of Monmouth).

-Basil Joseph Woollet died October 13th 1905 aged 44, (6 Agincourt Street, Monmouth). Other members of the Woollett family are also buried here.

-Matthew Bennett who died suddenly Aug 3 1917 aged 67yrs. Also his wife Sarah who ... died April 22 1915 aged 70 (Darren Cottage, Garway)

The death certificate of James Rosser of the New Inn, Skenfrith, (now The Sarn) who died in 30th October 1899, aged 84 is loose in the back of the Register.

vi
Registers for St Maughans Church

St Maughans was the parish church for the Hilston Park Estate, although not all those connected with the mansion house were buried there. Some of the relevant records that mention Hilston/Hillstone include:

General Register 1733-1813

Rev Thomas Phillips and Joyce,		married January 1733
Herbert,	son of Rev. Thomas Phillips,	baptised February 1735
Elizabeth,	dau. of Robert Needham	born August1740
Robert,	son of Robert Needham	was buried March 1748/49
Thomas,	son of Herbert Phillips	christened April 1766
James,	do.	baptised May1767
Catherine	do.	christened January 1769
Sarah	do.	christened November 1769
Charles	do.	baptised April 1771
William	do.	baptised March 1772
Susan	dau. of Mr Lambert of Hilston	christened November 1780
Nancy,	do.	christened November 1780
Catharina,	dau. of James Jones of Hillstone	baptised March 1782
Mary,	dau. of John Williams of Lower Hilston	baptised Jan 1785

John Francis Dormer, Romish Priest, brother to Lord Dormer, died at Upper Hillston and was buried in the chancil (sic) parish church of St Maughans, Feb 1770
Mr Robert Needham was buried 19th March 1769
Herbery Phillips Esq was buried 26th April 1801

Register of Marriages 1841-1968:
John Francis-Erskine, Earl of Mar, clerk in Holy Order, married Alice Hamilton of Hilston Park (daughter of John Hamilton)

Register of Baptisms 1813 onwards
James Evans of Hilston 1835
Frances Moore, daughter of George Cave Esq and Anne of Hilston 19th, September, 1841
Walter, son of George Cave, baptised 22nd October, 1844
William Chanders Brydges, baptised 11th October, 1874, son of William Henry Brydges, decorator to Gillow and Co. at Hilston Park

Register of Burials 1813 onwards
Rev. Charles Phillips   30.5.1813
Catherine Phillips   23.8.1818
Sir Robert Brownrigg   4.6.1833
Lady Sophia Brownrigg   5.5.1837 (of Bath, late of Hilston Park)
Frances Cave of Hilston 18months   20.2.1840
Charles Michell 24.4.1843 (Rev. of Monmouth)

vii
Landholdings of the Duchy of Lancaster - 1610

From a survey of the Duchy of Lancaster,
Lordships in Wales 1609-13.
Transcribed by William Rees 1953.

-Edward Lewys Miles; 1 messuage 1 barn 1 garden 1 orchard 15 acres land 15 acres of pasture formerly Wm Coxe   pays 6/-

-Thomas James Hilston; 8 acres arable and pasture in St Maughans, formerly James Hilston his father   pays 12d

-Richard and John Barry; 1 meadow called Garled Hilston containing 20 acres in St Maughan, formerly John Barry, their father pays 12d

APPENDIX

INDEX

Names in italics have their own chapter, but these references appear elsewhere in the book. Bold indicates the reference is non-textual and is a picture, a map or page from a catalogue

ted. Anders Franzén's purposeful researches and infectious enthusiasm, the skilled work of the divers and salvage teams, the lengthy toil of archaeologists, conservation experts, technicians, carpenters, art historians, riggers and many others have provided us all with a ship without equal in the world. Their achievement has been completed with the creation of a vigorous Vasa Museum of high architectonic content, a museum the outer form of which provides a vision of its contents. It is an exciting establishment where a great national and international public can meet, enjoy itself and learn. A museum in which the ship can live on – a living museum.

The Nordic museum and The Vasa Museum constitute an exciting constellation of the different ways two periods of time regard museum architecture; the one in the spirit of national romanticism at the end of the nineteenth century, and the other, opened in 1990, with form and function starting out from what the building is to contain. The stylised masts on the roof of the Vasa Museum demonstrate the dimensions of the fully-rigged Vasa.

can stimulate interest among the young, and the museum has devoted great interest in working with schools, direct teaching but also developing the educational side of museum activities.

Its position as one of Sweden's most important international tourist attractions marks many of the activities at the Vasa Museum, where multilingual information, guides and films in several languages as well as slide shows are available. Knowledge of and interest in the Vasa is great, a fact testified by the thousands and thousands of newspaper cuttings on the Vasa in all the languages of the world.

With the Vasa in place in her permanent museum, restored and with her lower standing rigging again in place, an epoch in the Vasa adventure has come to an end. With some confidence, this 1628 gem can be handed over to coming generations in the knowledge that the best conditions for the ship to be preserved have been crea-

**The sterncastle rises steeply above the upper deck.
Here are the gangways down to the steerage and the main cabin,
above the gangways to the upper cabin, and uppermost
the entrance to the poop-royal cabin.**

research work. At the same time, it became an excellent opportunity to hand practical knowledge of craftsmanship on to a younger generation. Today there are few opportunities to carry out in the seventeenth century manner such extensive rigging with its coarse and heavy cordage.

In February 1993, the foremast was lifted back on to the ship and in that same summer came the turn of the main mast. During the autumn the newly made mizzen mast was ready and put in place. In 1995 the rigging work was completed. With its lower standing rigging, the Vasa had now acquired the appearance ships overwintering in Stockholm had had in the Vasa's day, when everything loose in the rigging was taken down and stored.

The ship is a fascinating sight and an exciting experience to all her visitors. Most remarkable of all, of course, is to go on board and experience the singular atmosphere still remaining in this unique environment. For obvious reasons, however, it is not practicable to allow visitors on board. Between 750,000 and 800,000 people visit the museum every year. If these numbers were to go on to the ship, she would soon be worn out. To give the visitor some idea what it looked like on a gun-deck with guns in place in their gun carriages, the crew working and resting between the guns and the officers in the main cabin, have all been reflected in the exhibitions in a full-size replica of almost half the upper gun-deck – from the main mast and astern with the steerage and the admiral's cabin.

The Vasa is a creation that stimulates the imagination and becomes a great experience. But the value of the ship is increased by the complementary exhibitions. There are exhibitions showing the ship and her fate and adventures both in the seventeenth century and in our day. Also of Swedish society in the Vasa's day, life on board the ship, the symbolic language of the magnificent sculptures and the men behind it, on shipbuilding at Stockholm's shipyard where the Vasa was built, on the way a ship of this kind was sailed and how they found their way across the high seas.

The Vasa Museum is an obvious meeting point for all those interested in the sea, but also a place of great value for a multimillion public to visit, to find it exciting to make a closer acquaintance with the life, culture and history of the early seventeenth century. The museum is also working towards developing into a venue for the presentation of the art, theatre, music, dance and technology of the time. In changing temporary exhibitions and by public arrangements of various kinds, the Vasa Museum does not just claim to be a world class tourist attraction, but also functions as a centre to reflect an epoch in time and to contribute to making a section of history come alive in an increasingly history-less time. Not least, the Vasa

The major part of the carved decoration has been concentrated in the sterncastle, now restored in its entirity as in the original.

Towards her ultimate destination